REAL REVIVAL

REAL REVIVAL

by

Arthur L. Mackey, Jr.

ISBN 0-75960-584-X (soft cover)
ISBN 0-75960-585-8 (hard cover)
ISBN 0-75690-583-1 (Ebook)

This book is printed on acid free paper.

Mackey, Arthur L.
    Real Revival / Arthur L. Mackey, Jr., author and
illustrator. --1st ed.

    p. cm.
    Includes bibliographical references and index.
    1. Spiritual life--Christianity. 2. Religious
awakening--Christianity. 3. Revival. 4. Prayer--
Christianity. 5. Spiritual Healing. 6. Christian Life.
    I. Title.

BV4501.2.M33 2001   243
                QBI01-700247

1stBooks - rev. 11/14/01

Dedication

I dedicate this book to the loving memory of my father, the late Rev. Dr. Arthur L. Mackey Sr., Pastor Emeritus of the Mt. Sinai Baptist Church Cathedral in Roosevelt, New York.

I thank God for you being there for me as a father in everyday life and ministry. I will see you on the other side of glory. In the mean time, I will not forget the life lessons that you taught me through your powerful words and deeds, as well as through your keen sense of humor. You were a man of great excellence in Christ.

These are the characteristics that I will instill in my children.

REV. DR. ARTHUR L. MACKEY, SR.
Sunrise: April 29,1938 – Sunset: October 29, 1999

A Man of Purpose and Vision

Table of Contents

Acknowledgements

I would like to take this opportunity to express my gratitude to God, the Father, Son, and Holy Spirit, for inspiring me to write this book. Special thanks go to my wife, lover, and friend, First Lady Brenda Jackson Mackey, and my children, Yolanda, Jordan, and Faith. Thank you for your constant love and encouragement in the midst of some of life's greatest challenges that we faced together as husband and wife and family. To my mother and Church Administrative Assistant, Rev. Dr. Frances W. Mackey, President of the New York State Interdenominational Association of Minister's Wives and Widows, your wisdom, help, and assistance is greatly appreciated. Keep going on in Jesus name. Special thanks – to my sister, Frances Mackey Woodside, my brother-in-law, Elder Tyrone Woodside; to my sister, Vivian Mackey Johnson, my brother-in-law, Minister Moses Johnson, and; to Mr. Abraham and Rev. Bessie Jackson of Youngstown, Ohio; to Debbie Jackson Woodside, Patricia Jackson McClendon, Janet Jackson Smith, and Fannie Jackson, my sister-in-laws; my brother-in-law, James Smith; to my nieces and nephews, April, Shauna, Kwayn, and Kameisha; Amanda, Jonathan, Joshua, and Joel David; Chrissy, Alysa, Gerald, Tayleone, Pierre, James, Janet and Jaylen. Special thanks to the entire Mackey, Williams, and Jackson family. Special thanks to minister's wives and the ministerial staff, Dr. Mackey, Assistant to the Pastor, Rev. Willie R. Reid; Rev. John Williams, Minister Patricia Brown, Minister Kevin DeLee, Minister Samuel Garner, Minister Johnson, Minister Maurice Smith, and Minister Julia Weekfall. Special Thanks – to the greatest local church in the world, the entire membership and ministry leaders of the Mount Sinai Baptist Church Cathedral of Roosevelt, New York: to Deacon Board Chairman Deacon Aaron Scott, Jr. and Co-Chairman, Deacon Eddie Bryant and the Deacons; to Trustee Board Financial Chairman, Trustee Diane Womack, and Maintenance Chairman,

Trustee Leonard Yates, and the Trustees; Special thanks – to my mentor, Pastor Donnie McClurkin. Continue to touch the world for Jesus Christ through your pastoring, preaching, teaching, and singing. Your ministry is filling a major void in the lives of many. To Rev. Dr. Chris Tunde Joda thank you for writing the foreword to this book. To Elder Dorain Joyner of New Birth Missionary Baptist Church in Atlanta, Georgia. Thanks for being a brother from the days when first got saved and even up to right now. Your friendship is greatly valued and appreciated. To Norman Rohrer, Vanessa Robinson, and Lloyd Hilderbrand, thank you each for editing the manuscript. Special thanks to every book distributor, book buyer, and book reviewer. To Joni Blenn, thanks for all of your help. To Paul Bert, Candice McNeal and Charles Higgins of 1st Books, thank you for your help and assistance in putting this book out as an e-book, soft cover, hard cover, and audio-music book. Special thanks to George Greller of Barnes and Noble-B. Dalton, and all the Christian and secular bookstores for spreading the word concerning *Real Revival.*

Foreword

By Dr. Chris Tunde Joda
Christ Chapel International Churches
Lagos, Nigeria

I believe that this excellent book by Rev. Arthur Mackey Jr. will be a major catalyst in igniting revival in our world today.

David's cry to God in Psalm 85:6 is the same cry in the hearts of God's children today in this perplexing world. Too many things and situations are dead or decaying. We need life—the life of God that brings resurrection back to let the "dry bones" live again. This resurrection can come only by our experiencing real revival in our lives, in our families, in our finances and in our neighborhoods, as Rev. Mackey, Jr. rightly points out.

Revival is more than jumping or shouting—it is God's children living in a confident relationship with their God in today's world.

Real Revival expresses our revived faith in a living God—not a dead God of traditions and rules, but one who loves us deeply and wants to be relevant in every area of our lives today.

Rev. Mackey Jr. points out very glaringly the deficiencies and frustrations in trying to reach our world and proclaim the "good news" when we ourselves have not experienced this real revival.

This excellent book, which has been a product of more than seven years of searching and digging, is the deep cry of the heart of the author himself, whom I have known for several years.

In this book I am deeply inspired and touched by Rev. Mackey Jr.'s constant references to different revival cries from men of God in the Bible, from Ezra, from David, from Habbakuk and others. It is deep insight, the extent of which I have never seen.

Real Revival, says the author, sees a major move of God. And whenever you have a major move of God it effects not only the spiritual but also the physical, our finances, our emotions, and even our social relationships. Our God is a God who believes in wholeness and His revivals make us whole.

Real revival should be more than an event—monthly or even yearly. It should be daily—even hourly. Every dead area of our lives should be resurrected—our hopes, our dreams, our inspirations, our expectations, etc.

Thank you, Rev. Arthur Mackey Jr., for this soul-reviving and spirit-inspiring book. It has blessed my life and challenged me to look at a few more things in life closely and to make some deep decisions to go on with God.

This excellent book leaves readers with this question: "Will you be an active agent of revival in our world today?"

Say yes, and you will never regret it.

Introduction

WHY BELIEVERS NEED TO EXPERIENCE GENUINE REVIVAL
- Called to Be a Christian Witness in the Real World

Revived To Rejoice

Psalm 85 gives us the clearest reasons why we need to experience the real fire of revival. Psalm 85:6 asks, "Wilt thou not revive us again, that thy people may rejoice in thee?" That divine touch of genuine revival, which gives us true joy, is the same divine touch that gives us inner strength to face and overcome our deepest fears in this journey called life. Rejoicing is not just a matter of jumping and shouting for joy; it is in a far greater sense the difference between spiritual life and death, revival or ruin.

One of the main purposes for revival's fresh fire is that the people of God may freely rejoice in God again, even in the midst of life's raging storms. David Bryant, founder and president of Concerts of Prayer International, stated in an article entitled "Prisoners of Hope" that "Large segments of the church have been taken captive by God to the radical hope of personal and corporate revival. It is cause for Christians to rejoice, knowing from history that great advances in the mission of the church have come in such seasons of spiritual awakening and renewal."[1]

As believers, we must never minimize the potency of the joy of the Lord for it is our very strength. A Christian who lacks joy is also a Christian who lacks strength for the journey. We will revisit this road to real rejoicing in much more detail in chapter four. How many times do we begin to lose the joy of our salvation in the midst of the daily hustle and bustle routines of real life in a real world full of real challenges. Clearly Nehemiah taught that in spite of it all "The joy of the Lord is our strength." When we worship and praise God, the heart of God becomes joyful. In turn He gives us strength for the problems, predicaments, and precarious situations of real life. This is the very core essence of real revival that brings our dead spiritual relationship with the Almighty God back to life.

This is true resurrection power that calls the saints of God into the fellowship of His suffering. This is the point where cowardly Christian soldiers are radically transformed into men of war trained by the Master to be armed and dangerous in the realm of the spirit, and prepared for the challenge in the natural realm. Real revival endows the Christian believer with strength to make it through the struggle, through the pain, and through the heartache. Strength to reach the battered, broken, and bruised in Jesus name. Strength to reach our children in the community, our sons and daughters, nieces, nephews, and cousins in Jesus's name with a message of real revival.

In his book *Children of Revival: Letting the Little Ones Lead*, Vann Lanes writes: "I believe the children of the inner city will become our next 'children of revival.' They will experience the power and presence of Jesus and, as a result, they will lead their peers and parents to Him."[2] Psalm 85:6 points it out very clearly: "Wilt thou not revive us again, that thy people may rejoice in thee?" The writer of Psalm 85, "the chief musician," who was originally writing a psalm for the sons of Korah, is also giving us the answer for the sons and daughters of today's society, that God wants children, youth, young adults, adults, and senior citizens to receive the last days' outpouring of real revival that we might rejoice in Him in the worst and best of times. We are chosen by the Creator God to be true Christian witnesses to the real world to which they respond by crying, "Wow! This blows my mind. The church is finally on fire with real revival that impacts lives of hurting people in the community." This won't occur without a deep relationship that includes intense, intimate worship and praise to God. So we will not lose the joy of our salvation, our first true lover of the soul—today, here and now. Jesus's joy is not based on what is happening. In his book *Jesus, Man of Joy,* Sherwood Eliot Wirt, founding editor of *Decision* magazine states, that "God offers us inner joy here on earth and forever after through Jesus Christ. Do we have it? I don't mean happiness. Happiness has been defined as the look on a dieter's face on reaching the desired weight and heading for a restaurant. Inner joy is something different. It's there between meals."[3]

The joy of Jesus in our hearts is built on the solid foundation that we have hope in God concerning the forgiveness of our past, power for our present situation, and faith for our future. This joy that I have the world did not give it to me, and the world can't take it away. Our Christian joy is a clarion witness in the midst of pain, problems, and predicaments, to the real world that God, the Healer of the wounded soul, is still on the throne even in the midst of life's worst setbacks.

In her foreword to the late Rev. Dr. Samuel DeWitt Proctor's classic book, *The Substance of Things Hoped For*, Marian Wright Edelman, President of the Children's Defense Fund, wrote: "We must reach out most of all to children and commit to mentoring and healing. And we must understand that the solutions lie in family, education, wise public policy, and a return to moral values that are lived and not just preached."[4]

Yes, real revival that addressees the hard core, down to earth, jagged edged issues of real life is the only experience that can turn the hearts of the fathers to the children, and the hearts of the children to the fathers, lest God smite the earth with a curse for the sin of ignoring the children and their destiny in Christ.

Revival is a much needed reality check that it is time to die to the demonic control of the flesh, and yield to the power of the Holy Spirit. We must boldly share this real revival message with the sons and daughters of today. Real Revival brings the backslidden believer as the Old Testament would say, or the "carnally minded," as the New Testament would say, back to the fullness of life in, and a love affair with, Christ.

In *Digging the Wells of Revival,* Lou Engle states that "Covenant love is what revival is all about. It is not about restoring old practices and methods or re-establishing old traditions. We are seeking to restore the original heart motivations and sacrificial love that moved God to act in revival power in the past. 'He will restore the hearts of the fathers to their children, and the hearts of the children to the fathers' (Mal. 4:6a NAS)is the watchword and promise."[5]

Real revival is being consumed by the power of His resurrection and by the fellowship of His sufferings. Real revival never begins until the two edged sword of God's word cuts our sinful life right where it hurts the most, for we are called to be a Christian witness in a real world with real problems. You cannot be revived unless you first die to the selfish philosophy of me, myself, and I in the process of crying out to God with a truly repentant heart, thereby becoming a candidate for the power of His resurrection and the fellowship of His suffering. Rev. Dr. Martin Luther King, Jr., the late leader of the nationwide civil rights revival in the 1950's and 60's that was literally birthed by the power of persistent prayer, said that "an individual has not started living until he can rise above the narrow confines of individualistic concerns to the broader concerns of humanity."[6]

Now, of course, when you look at Psalm 30, this real revival message is backed up. Psalm 30, and verse 4, says, "Sing unto the Lord, ye saints of His, and give thanks at the remembrance of His holiness." Now listen to this in the 5th verse. This is very familiar: "For His anger endureth but a moment; in His favor is life: Weeping may endure for a night, but joy cometh in the morning." In the favor of God there is life. In the favor of God there is resurrection power. In the favor of God there is real revival from deep spiritual and moral decay. The joy of Jesus that gives us strength for the journey is the source of courage to share our Christian witness with the real world that is full of real life challenges, and is in search of God.

The world is searching for God in all the wrong places today--witchcraft, physics, fortune tellers, etc. The world needs revived Christians whose lives are a living testimony that points the lost to the redemptive cross of Christ. Genuine revival is a constant reality check up that calls holiness to our remembrance. Genuine revival resurrects the backslidden believer, the carnal Christian from the dead, and boldly proclaims that in His favor is life. In His favor, God's favor, is resurrection power even after Mary and Martha have wept all night long. Weeping may endure for a night, but joy, resurrection joy, and real revival joy come in the morning.

Remember, real revival teaches us to rejoice in God in both good and bad times, so that we don't lose the joy of our salvation. The joy of the Lord must not be mistaken for a negative, evasive, and weak form of Christianity that totally ignores the real issues of life in the human drama. Joy is different from happiness. Happiness is based upon what is happening at the time, but joy can be experienced even when everything is going wrong.

Help! We Need Revival

Now listen to verse 10-12 of Psalm 30: "Hear, O Lord, and have mercy upon me: Lord, be thou my helper." Clearly now we're beginning to see the connection in scripture of God being our focus. When we're saying, "Folk, we need Holy Ghost fire revival," we're recognizing and acknowledging the fact that God is our helper, always. And always remember that the only way we will experience it is by seeking the face of God and not by seeking the experience of revival in and of itself. He helps us by leading us into the realm of real revival and restoration.

Dr. Ben Carson, the world renowned pediatric neurosurgeon who successfully separated Siamese twins who were connected at the head, wrote in his book *Think Big: Unleashing Your Potential for Excellence,* that "If we acknowledge our need for God, He will help us."[7]

Psalm 30:10 says, "Lord, be thou my helper," and then it goes on in verse 11 to say, "Thou has turned for me my mourning into dancing:" Okay, that's real revival fire right there. "That He has turned for me my mourning," the state of mourning, deep sympathy, and heavy sorrow, "into dancing"--a state of joy that only Jesus Christ can give. Ecstasy in Him, yes in Christ. Great pleasure even in the midst of pain and pressure. That represents and constitutes real revival, a genuine movement of God's Spirit in the earth today in times of crisis.

Going from the point of mourning to dancing is a major change, a major turning point that constitutes genuine revival, for only Jesus can make a deep mourner into a dancer in the midst of a mess.. And now this, of course, is a personal revival (my mourning into dancing). This is speaking about an individual, but once the writer of Psalm 85 shared it with others it became a corporate revival with a worldwide impact. The message has survived. It is still spreading like wild fire. This real revival message is a solid Christian witness to the real world that our God cares for His children, even when we are at our lowest points. We need to experience the true meaning of the genuine revival experience because if our gospel be hid then it is hid to them who are lost.

Gird Me With Gladness

Psalm 85 goes on to say, "Thou hast put off my sackcloth, and girded me with gladness."

The 12th verse adds, "To the end that my glory may send praise to thee, and not be silent." In other words, God doesn't want us to lose that joy of our salvation. The joy of the Lord is our strength. So He's giving us this glory to praise Him and magnify His Name so that we don't have to sit in silence in the midst of our struggle.

And then it adds, "O Lord my God, I will give thanks unto thee forever." True revival brings forth the committed life, a lifestyle where the grace of God is flowing, and where the grace of God leads into holiness--a totally committed Christian lifestyle that helps us to overcome the constant barrage of temptation in the real world. Without real revival the church is dead, dull and void of divine destiny and direction. Pastor Donnie McClurkin of Perfecting Faith Church in Freeport, New York hits the nail directly on the head of the real revival move of God message when he ministers so powerfully the song "We Fall Down, but we get up." Real Revival tells the fallen brother or sister that we can get back up again.

J. I. Packer gives the following definition of revival: "Revival I define as a work of God by His Spirit through His Word, bringing the spiritually dead to living faith in Christ and renewing the inner life of Christians who have grown slack and sleepy. In revival God makes old things new, giving new power to law and gospel and new spiritual awareness to those whose hearts and consciousnesses have become blind, hard and cold. Revival thus animates or re-animates churches and Christian groups to make a spiritual and moral impact on communities. It comprises an initial reviving, followed by a maintained state of revivedness for as long as the visitation lasts."

Clearly, in the 10th and 11th verses, we see the connection between revival and God as our ever-present helper. It is important that we recognize God's help in our life so we can cry, "Help! We need revival in our homes, in our relationships, in our marriages and finances. Help! I am dying on the inside. I deeply need to be recharged, refreshed, renewed, restored, and revived in my life, in my dying marriage, and my dysfunctional home. Without a touch of real revival, I am sunk. I cannot go on one second more without a touch from you, God, in my daily condition of existence. It's clear that we're not talking about something that's impossible. The scripture clearly teaches that God is our helper in this journey called life. God wants to bring healing in the home and marriage.

In her book, "Help Me, I'm Married!" noted author and conference speaker, Joyce Meyer clearly points out the need for real revival in marriage. God helps us by teaching us that "faith without works is dead." Mrs. Meyer states that "Good marriages are not an accident. If you want to have a great relationship with anyone, you have to work at it." Mrs. Meyer goes on to further state, "Go to dinner and perhaps, occasionally, stay in a nice hotel, even if it is close to home. Don't let your life get boring! There are so many people who are just bored with their lives. Do something about boredom! Be creative! Pray and ask God for ideas...Protect these outings between the two of you. Be sure they happen frequently enough to keep your outlook stirred with new scenery. Go out every one or two weeks and discover what it's like just to be in each other's company. Hold hands, rub shoulders, hug and show respect to each other. Demonstrate to the world what God's love looks like between two people."[8]

"Hear, oh Lord, and have mercy upon me, Lord. Be thou my helper." Jesus Christ, the anointed One, the Lord of Revival, is my Help to deal with the real issues of life and get victory in everyday real life situations. Help for real life situations such a troubled marriage, divorce, depression, despair, and death. Jesus Christ is the power source for deep, inner healing, essential wholeness from the wounds of the past, and problems of the present. Now He's turned my mourning into dancing. He has put off my sackcloth and girded me with gladness. That's real revival in the midst of the storm.

Hebrews 13:6 backs this up also: "So that we may boldly say, The Lord is my helper, I will not fear what man shall do unto me." So when we say, "Help, we need real revival," it's teaching us that we can boldly say that the Lord is our helper even when we feel hopeless. Jesus Christ, the Lord of Revival is my source of help. God wants us to come boldly before the throne of grace to call upon His Name, even in the time of need. The ultimate arrogance is to say, "Well, I have enough revival in my life. I don't need to say, 'Help! I need real revival in every single area of life,' because I'm experiencing enough revival. I've been to the best crusade, or I've been to the best conventions." That's the ultimate arrogance. Why do we need real revival? Because without it the church is lifeless, powerless, and hopeless. Why do we need real revival? Because the church is stuck in the grave of unconfessed sin. It is in drastic need of daily repentance.

The Bible says, "Humble yourself," not with phony humbling, but with the real thing that the Bible talks about. "Humble yourself under the mighty hand of God that He will exalt you in due time."

So clearly, scripture teaches that the Lord is my helper my Refresher, my Renewer, my Restorer, my Revitalizer, my Reviver, and my Redeemer from the curse of the law. Jesus Christ is the Lord of Revival. In the living class entitled "The Quest for Revival-Experiencing Great Revival of the Past, Empowering You For God's Move Today!" Author Ron McIntosh states that, "Revival is the revitalization of the Church for a divine attack on society. Revival is the marshalling of forces fatal to the Kingdom of darkness. Revival is the enlisting, training, and empowering of believers as a prelude to evangelization. Revival is God's military tactic that concentrates His resources for a vital blow at a crucial moment. Revival is that which reinvigorates God's people with His truth and power."We need His help because there is no hope without all of our help coming from the Lord of Revival. Also we must realize that not only is Jesus our help, our advocate who is on the right hand of the Father, but the Holy Spirit is also our help, our advocate here on earth. He is the *Parakletos*, a Greek word meaning, one who is called alongside to help us, our advocate on earth, our attorney. The Holy Spirit is our comforter. God the Father is also our help. He's a Father to the fatherless. If your father has died, He's there for you. If he's still alive but he's not around, God is a Father to the fatherless.

And the word also says that He is a judge to the widows. So there's a woman and she's been abused by the husband, the husband is not there, God is a judge to the widows, He's the one who will bring justice to your situation, and He's the one who will bless you and bring you out of the hardship that you're going through, yes Lord. So we must realize that God is our helper, God the Father, God the Son and God the Holy Spirit.

Jesus Christ, the Lord of Revival, wants to help us through timeless wisdom of the Heavenly Father, and the anointing of the Holy Spirit to develop a powerful Christian witness to the real world.

A Little Reviving in Our Bondage

Two of the key scriptures that best exemplify the message, "Help, we need real revival" are found in Ezra 9:8. The latter part of verse 8 says, "Our God makes light in our eyes, and gives us a little reviving in our bondage." Why do we need to experience real revival? Because it teaches us that God can raise us up from the dead, and give us life even in our bondage and totally deliver us from our bondage.

Look at the language of that text, "Give us a little reviving in our bondage." Evidently, Ezra was aware that there was a problem. Now Ezra experienced a great revival and the people that Ezra preached to experienced a great revival. But I'm encouraged by his honesty in dealing with the problem. "A little reviving in our bondage"--this is a believer who is praying. This is a man who knows God, who walks closely with God, but yet he says, "Give us a little reviving on our bondage."

He didn't say, "Give us a little reviving in *their* bondage." He said, "Give us a little reviving in *our* bondage." He realized that he just got a little touch from the Lord of Revival, just a tap on the finger from God would be enough to release or deliver all of the folk in bondage, all of the people in bondage.

I can appreciate that type of honesty. In many cases you don't see that in today's world or even in the church, but that's what we need, that type of honesty: "Help, we need real revival! Give us a little reviving in our bondage." We will look into this teaching point with more in-depth focus in chapter one.

Revive Thy Work

Let's look at Habakkuk the 3rd chapter and the 2nd verse. The prophet says "Oh Lord, I have heard thy speech and was afraid." He admits that he was afraid. "God hasn't given us the spirit of fear, but of power, and of love and of a sound mind." But this fear was more a respect for what God had said. He wanted an awesome, sovereign move of God, a genuine revival, a time of refreshing sent from the presence of the Lord. Of course he was going to do his part. He was a praying man, a man of great faith, deep love, abiding trust in God, but yet he had a fear, a respect and reverence for God.

He says, "Oh Lord, I have heard thy speech and was afraid. Oh Lord, revive thy work." Habakkuk was a great prophet. God put a great calling on his life.

God has to revive the work. We cannot revive the work, we cannot manufacture real revival, and we cannot make it happen. We have to humble ourselves, we have to seek His face, we have to turn from our wicked ways. Then will He hear from heaven. Then will He forgive our sins, and will heal our land. The Holy Spirit draws us and empowers and enables us to repent.

We can do that because He chose us in the first place. He created us and He ordained us. So, whatever we can do is a privilege, but we can't manufacture a genuine revival. The only thing that we can do is what He has allowed us to do, and what He has told us to do. When we do that, we're obedient.

But he goes on and says, "Oh Lord, I have heard thy speech and was afraid. Oh Lord, revive thy work in the midst of the years." In other words, he realizes that God used revival in the past. Lord of Revival, Dear Jesus, you can do it again because it's your work. That's the key to genuine revival. That's the key to show that revival is a sovereign move of God, but we have our part to contribute in terms of prayer.

The bottom line is that it's God's work but you have a part to share. If you think it's your work it's not going to work. It's not going to happen. But when you realize that it's God's work it becomes evident that this is a sovereign move of God. He can send real revival. He can answer prayer because we did it the right way, God's way. Real revival opens the eyes of the spiritually blinded. Real revival gives the people of God purpose and vision, and without a vision the people perish.

In his book entitled, *Revival Fire,* Wesley Duewel states that "revival days are not normal days in the life of the church. They are supernormal, supernatural. They are the great days of the church when God manifests His presence in overwhelming reality. They leave you with a profound realization of God's greatness and transcendence and of your own unworthiness and dependence on Him." [9]

"Revive thy work in the midst of the years." Now listen to this. It says, "In the midst of the years, make known in wrath, remember mercy." So the prophet Habakkuk understood clearly that there are a lot of things that God can be angry about. There are a lot of things in our world today that God can be angry about. But we have to pray, "In wrath, remember mercy." We will discuss this aspect of revival in more detail in chapters five and eight.

Candidates for Real Revival

A lot of times we say, "But revival is for the church," and that is true. We talk about revival like we're talking about evangelism. In all reality, evangelism is the baby that real revival gives birth to. But one thing I think people fail to realize is that the church is much larger than what we think. When we talk about the church many times, people just remit to their charismatic clan. Or they limit it to their evangelical enclave, or their Baptist brethren, or the Lutheran list, or their Methodist mission. But the body of Christ is much broader than that. There are people who have a love for God, but might be in a backslidden condition.

Most of them are candidates for real revival because they're backslidden Christians. They may not be witnessing to anybody. They may not be sharing the gospel with anybody, but they've been saved before. There are more people than what we would acknowledge, who are real candidates for revival. So when we're saying, "Help, we need revival," I'm not just talking about a revival in one city, I'm talking about a worldwide revival, a revival that has a local impact. But from local impact it spreads to worldwide revival. This is a daily revival for persecuted Christians in foreign nations who are being mutilated for the cause of Christ. This is a daily revival for the rape victim who yearns to get the victory even in the middle of the mess. This is a daily revival for the poor man and the rich man. As I said before, there are more people than you would ever imagine who are candidates for real revival. Why do we need to experience real revival? Because God is our only hope. Nobody but Jesus can turn your life around.

Winkie Pratney in his book "Revival-It's Principles and Personalities- Twenty Centuries of Vision and Visitation" makes a statement that is still relevant in the 21st Century. Pratney states that, "The Spirit of revival is the consciousness of God...... It is God's moving in power and holiness toward you and calling your name!"

Anybody who has ever heard the gospel, and has confessed Jesus with their mouth, and believed in their heart that He is risen from the dead and has ever sinned, is a candidate for real revival. That's a lot of people--more people than you could ever imagine. God is calling your name. God is calling their name. God is calling your name. God is calling my name. God has a personal revival with your name on it. In fact, that includes every Christian who is alive.

So when we talk about real revival we cannot limit ourselves. There are different aspects of revival. The only aspects that we have really looked into with great detail are the meetings. We really haven't begun to look at how this revival can touch the lives of ordinary people, because that's the revival that continues. That's the revival that lasts. That's the revival that births evangelism. Yes, that is the real revival for troubled times in which God calls the Christian Church to be a bold witness to the real world. "For if our gospel be hid, it is hid to them who are lost."

Arthur L. Mackey, Jr.

Continuous Revival

Now the meetings, Azusa street and all the great revivals, didn't last forever, but we will be talking about their positive impact even on the other side of glory. I'm talking about revival that *can* last for eternity, as far as its impact on society is concerned. Once it is over, the rapture happens. Being with Jesus for eternity is the ultimate revival. Being changed in a moment, in the twinkling of an eye, and being caught up to meet Jesus, the Lord of Revival, in the air is the ultimate "revival". Having our mortal bodies changed into immortality is the ultimate revival, for our salvation and deliverance is in its fullness. And if you don't think it's possible, I'm here to let you know that it is possible. It's the revival that God does in your life; it's something that can constantly be renewed day by day. We're in this molded body. For every day that we move and function as human beings, we're actually dying daily. But if we could be renewed in the spirit of our mind, "Be not conformed to this world, but be transformed by the renewing of your mind," and allow it to be renewed day by day, we can get into a state of revival that would go on.

I'm reminded of the saying by Vance Havner: "Revival is the church falling in love with Jesus all over again."[1] That's why we talk about the quest for spiritual renewal. As you tie spiritual renewal in with the real revival, you can experience a continuous revival. And if you can experience real, genuine revival in your personal life, and you share it with others, then they can experience this continuous revival on a corporate level. And I'm not talking about revival in the sense of a meeting. More importantly, I'm talking about the plain experience that the Bible talks about, being renewed in the spirit of our mind, day by day. I'm talking about changed lives. Drug users and Drug dealers who have been delivered and are now preaching the gospel of Jesus Christ and raising healthy families.

But if we're really honest, we all have problems and we all have struggles. We talk about mismanaged finances and bad unfruitful and unhealthy relationships. We talk about giving up things. Yes, these issues can be overwhelming. But God can give you the victory over these as well as other problems. I'm referring to problems that seem monumental in nature. The point that I'm making is that the Lord of Revival, Jesus Christ, the Anointed, who is our Help, will teach us how to handle the inconveniences of life. How we respond to problems is the basis of our Christian witness to the world that we have been quickened, stirred up, and revived to survive the storm.

No matter what is going on with a person, regardless if they are rich, poor, or middle class, there is always going to be some struggle that they have to deal with. And that's not a bad confession. It's a reality of life. But remember, we can speak the word of Jesus, our Help, the Lord of Revival, and overcome the problem, predicaments, and precarious situations in the home, in the church, and in the community.

World Wide Revival

So when you look at it in that context, it's not such a bad thing. Above all, we must realize what God is trying to do in these last days, He wants to pour out His Spirit upon all flesh. All flesh. Black flesh. White flesh. Yellow flesh. Brown flesh. All flesh that truly is yielded to the Heavenly Father shall be touched by the Reviver Himself, Jesus, the Christ. A lot of people haven't heard the gospel yet. He wants the knowledge of His Word to cover this whole world, as the waters cover the sea. Real world-wide revival always starts right where you are at. That is God's bottom line. He makes that very clear in the book of Habakkuk. God wants the knowledge of His Word to cover this whole earth, and get to every person, as the waters cover the sea.

And that takes a worldwide revival. It starts where you are right now. It starts in your Jerusalem. It starts in your upper room then it spreads like wild fire. So if we can just get out of our spiritual arrogance, and focus on the need for real revival throughout the world and in the church, I know God will honor our praise, worship, and submission to Him.

I've often heard people say, "This is going on in that city, that's going on in this city." All of that is great, but it's nothing compared to what God wants to do. We need to participate and celebrate the move of God. It will be the catalyst to motivate us in the 21st Century. We need to be like God the Father who is a Father to the fatherless. As was stated earlier, God the Father desires to turn the hearts of the fathers to the children, and the hearts of the children to the fathers through the message of real revival. These factors will bring heritage and restoration back to families that have been separated and torn apart. Jesus, my Lord of Revival, you're my helper. "Help me, Holy Spirit, you're my comforter, you're my peace, and you're my advocate. Holy Spirit, my Comforter, you are called along side to help me, you are my source of deep inner healing."

When we are honest with God, God will help us. He will bring real, genuine revival to our lives. He will revive our quest, our search, our journey for spiritual renewal. God will begin to renew our spirit, mind, and body. For I am a spirit. I have a soul. I live in a body.

The Glory of the Latter House

In Haggai 2:9 he says, "The glory of the latter house shall be greater than the former." That's a true statement, the glory of the latter house shall be greater than the former. No matter what has happened in your past, God is saying that the glory of your latter house will be greater than the former. Your past does not control, nor does it equal, your future. But the glory of the latter house should be greater than the former. We will discuss the glory of the latter house and its relevance to the real revival experience in more detail in chapter 12.

You may have been a drug addict. You may have been a convict. You may have been an alcoholic. There is something that God is trying to reveal to you. Behold, God wants to do a new work in you. He wants to make a way in your wilderness, but you have to yield to that and realize that your best days are ahead.

Just be honest with God and say, "Help, Abba Father." Realize that God is our Father, "Abba Father, I need your help." Big Daddy, I need your heavenly wisdom to be an effective Christian witness in this real world with real problems. Why do we need to experience real revival? Because without it, God-given opportunities for effective evangelism would never be birthed through the portal of purpose into reality.

And He will come. He who comforts, no matter what pain you struggle with, He'll be there. He said, "Lo, I'll be with you always, even unto the end of the world." He said, "I'll never leave you nor forsake you, I'll be right by your side."

Standing in the Gap

In the early part of October 1997, prior to my trip to Lagos, Nigeria, I had the honor and privilege of going with my father, the late Rev. Arthur L. Mackey, Sr., to the Promise Keepers "Standing In The Gap" meeting. I cherish this ministry trip even more since the recent passing away of my father. It was a sacred gathering of men from all over the nation and the world held in Washington, D.C. We were accompanied by brother Donald Hatcher, our Minister of Music at Mt. Sinai Baptist Church; Trustee Clifton Jones the President of our Transportation Committee; Trustee Leonard Yates, Maintenance Chairman of The Trustee Board; Deacon Curtis Womack, President of our Men's ministry and Superintendent of our Sunday School; Brother David Todd and his son, David, and Brother Sam Hall. My good friend, Karl Droesler, also attended the event. He brought his wheelchair with him. We went on what was called

"The Gospel Express," an Amtrak train leaving from New York's Penn Station bound for Washington, D.C.

When we arrived at the meeting location, which was at the Washington Monument, I saw a gathering of men. It was tremendous. The service had just started. As far as the eye could see, from the Capitol to the Washington Monument, from the Lincoln Memorial and beyond, all you could see were men....

Speaker after speaker dealt with the subject of revival which helped me to recognize what God was trying to do. The worship and praise really brought into focus the awesome presence of God. To look around to see thousands and thousands of men get down on their knees and pray before God was a heavenly vision. It was a sight that was almost unbelievable. This was an experience that was highly motivating, because it prepared my heart for the move of God in Lagos, Nigeria.

Why do we need real revival? Because we cannot survive without true times of refreshing sent straight from the very throne room presence of the Lord.

The men that were there were crying out to God. Seeking His face and not His hand. Men from all walks of life, just crying out to God for revival. In essence they were crying out, "Help, God! I need you! I need you to take control of my job, my marriage, and my home. Help me to deal with my children. I need your guidance."

With all the arrogance that I have seen and heard, I didn't see or hear it there. Instead, I heard a genuine cry for real revival. And what I would say is: We need more of that. We just can't stop with that one meeting, because that meeting, of course, really was not about Promise Keepers and the seven promises of Promise Keepers. That meeting was actually about real revival. Thank God that Promise Keepers hosted the meeting and organized the meeting, but it went beyond an individual organization. It was a genuine move of God.

A Genuine Move of God

And that's what we need, a genuine move of God. Yes, as I said many times in the book already, our part is that we have to pray a deeply burning and fervent prayer. Pray and use the P.U.S.H. method - Pray until something happens. Now please remember, praising God for what you pray for is extremely important. Pray until there is a sovereign move of God in which the fire of the Holy Ghost empowers the church to crusade the lost world as though it was their last chance before the last call. I'll repeat it because repetition is the mother of all skills: hopefully somebody will pick this up: God wants us to humble ourselves and pray, seek His face, turn from our wicked ways. Then He will hear from heaven. Then He will forgive our sin, and then, and only then, He will heal our land. Then He will bring real revival. Why do we need to experience real revival? Because it is the work of God, and not the hype of man.

Remember Habakkuk: "Revive thy works." It's His work, so it's a sovereign move of God. Since He's the only one who can really heal the land, it's a sovereign move of God. We cannot manufacture real revival. The only thing that we can do is what He allows us to do. God has empowered us by His Holy Spirit to humble ourselves, pray, seek His face and turn from our wicked ways. Then will He hear from heaven, forgive our sins, and heal the land.

We can't manufacture real revival. We can only do what He has asked us to do in the first place, or ordained for us and to do it well. And when we do it, then we're in obedience to Him, but we can't manufacture it. We can't make it happen in the sense of that statement of doing it our own way with the philosophy of me, myself and I. The only thing that we can do is get in line with His program because it's a sovereign move of God. If we truly pray a deeply burning and fervent prayer of revival fire he will tell us what to do and how to plan so we flow in His pressence with perfected praise and divine purpose.

Arthur L. Mackey, Jr.

That day in the Capital I saw God do something. And as we were leaving to come back to New York, and the men were heading to different trains, there were protesters in the train station. They were yelling out different types of slurs at us. But then the men began to sing, "What a Mighty God We Serve, angels bow before Him, heaven and earth adore Him, what a mighty God we serve." The men came together. Men began to sing in the train station in Washington, D.C. Ironically, many of the protesters pulled down their signs and began to sing with the men. It was real revival, a genuine experience, more than just a mass meeting.

Protesters who were against the "Promise Keepers" called us sexist. Many of the protesters were people who grew up and went to somebody's church. By the grace of God, they threw down their signs. They remembered those songs that they sang when they were growing up. They remembered the prayers and they began to think: *Hey, we're not on different sides. We're on the same side. The only thing that we need to do is repent and get right with God and realize that we're on the same team.* Many of those people did repent, but some didn't. Some continued to protest, but there were people in the train station that day who gave their lives to the Lord. Their lives were changed forever. I thank God for that type of experience. I thank God, because that represents genuine revival--not revival in the sense of some big meeting that may last seven, eight or nine years. But it was a revival that will last forever, as long as those people renew their mind to the power of God's Word daily. It will last for eternity. Why do we need to experience real revival? Because without it we can not know God in the power of His resurrection and the fellowship of His suffering.

That's the type of revival we're looking for. Keep it real! Real, authentic revival that begins in the heart of one person and spreads like wild fire throughout the world. A real, genuine revival that's not controlled by one man, one woman, or one church. But it's a real revival that's controlled by the Spirit of God that comes upon all flesh, male and female, in all colors, and flavors of life, that nobody controls. Oh yes, God allows this real revival flame to spread like wild fire in the dry woods full of trees.

In the epilogue we will look at the call of Christ to keep the fire burning in more detail. Read and be blessed. Why do we need so desperately to experience real revival? Because we very well might be the only example of the love of Jesus that some people will ever experience. We are called to experience real revival in order for God to enlighten us, endow us from on high, and empower us to be a positive Christian witness to the real world that we live in. We need real revival because each day we are one day closer to death. Therefore we are constantly in the need of revival for the spirit, soul, and body, as we prepare for the other side of this journey called life.

If you can plan it out, it is not real revival. If you can organize it to fit man's agenda, it is not real revival. If you give up your plans for His plans. Give up your fleshly purpose for His divine purpose, and give up your agenda for His agenda. Then you are on the right road to real revival. Real revival is birthed from the loins of genuine repentance. Merely seeking revival does not cause real revival fire to fall on the church. Rather, seeking God Himself with fervent, unending passion for the presence of Christ in our lives causes real revival fire to fall afresh on us from above.

Arthur L. Mackey, Jr.

PART ONE:

THE PURPOSE OF REVIVAL

Chapter 1

BELIEVERS, WE NEED REAL REVIVAL
--A SOVEREIGN MOVE OF GOD

Ezra's Prayer

"And at the evening sacrifice I rose up from my heaviness; and having rent my garment and my mantle, I fell upon my knees, and spread out my hands unto the Lord my God. And said, O my God, I am ashamed and blush to lift up my face to thee my God: for our iniquities are increased over our head, and our trespass is grown up unto the heavens."

"Since the days of our fathers we have been in a great trespass unto this day; and for our iniquities have we, our kings, and our priests, been delivered into the hands of the kings of the lands, to the sword, to captivity, and to a spoil, and to confusion of face, as it is this day. And now for a little space grace hath been shewed from the Lord our God, to leave us a remnant to escape, and to give us a nail in His holy place, that our God may lighten our eyes, and give us a little reviving in our bondage.

"For we were bondsmen; yet our God hath not forsaken us in our bondage, but hath extended mercy unto us in the sight of the kings of Persia, to give us a reviving, to set up the house of our God, and to repair the desolation thereof, and to give us a wall in Judah and in Jerusalem."

"And now, O our God, what shall we say after this? for we have forsaken thy commandments, which thou hath commanded by thy servants the prophets, sayings, The land, unto which ye go to possess it, is an unclean land with the filthiness of the people of the lands, with their abominations, which have filled it from one end to another with their uncleanness."

"Now therefore give not your daughters unto their sons, neither take their daughters unto your sons, nor seek their peace or their wealth for ever: that ye may be strong, and eat the good of the land, and leave it for an inheritance to your children for ever. And after all that is come upon us for our evil deeds, and for our great trespass, seeing that thou our God hath punished us less than our iniquities deserve, and hath given us such deliverance as this;"

"Should we again break thy commandments, and join in affinity with the people of these abominations? Wouldest not thou be angry with us till thou hadst consumed us, so that there should be no remnant nor escaping? O Lord God of Israel, thou art righteous; for we remain yet escaped, as it is this day; behold, we are before thee in our trespasses; for we cannot stand before thee because of this" (Ezra 9:5-15).

Let's take a closer look at verses 8 and 9 in Ezra 9: "And now for a little space grace hath been shewed from the Lord our God, to leave us a remnant to escape, and to give us a nail in His holy place, that our God may lighten our eyes, and give us a little reviving in our bondage. For we were bondsmen; yet our God hath not forsaken us in our bondage, but hath extended mercy unto us in the sight of the kings of Persia, to give us a reviving, to set up the house of our God, and to repair the desolation thereof, and to give us a wall in Judah and in Jerusalem."

Revival Begins with Prayer

The revival that the Prophet Ezra declares is what we need today. His prayer is simply stated: "Help, we need revival. Help, we need revival." This should be our prayer today as well.

It is a prayer that was echoed by the Prophet Habakkuk: "O Lord, I have heard thy speech, and was afraid: O Lord, revive thy work in the midst of the years, in the midst of the years make known; in wrath remember mercy" (Hab. 3:2).

God wants to bring revival to His people and to our land. Revival must be bathed in prayer, just as both Ezra and Habakkuk reveal. In order to relate to revival we must understand its meaning. Winkie Pratney gives a clear definition in the book, *Revival: Its Principles & Personalities* (Huntington House Publishers, Lafayette, Louisiana): "Revival means to reanimate, renew, awaken, re-invigorate, restore; to make the church whole and happy in God again. Revival is more than big meetings, religious excitement, a quickening of the saints, being filled with the Holy Spirit, or great harvest of souls. One may have one or all of these without revival."[1]

Ezra -- a Great Prayer Warrior

The Book of Ezra is a very interesting book. It is written by a man who is not a Bible personage with whom most of us are very familiar. Ezra is seldom regarded as one of the great Bible heroes that we talk about. We talk and preach about Moses, we talk and preach about David, and we talk about the apostles Paul and Peter. But seldom do we hear of the great exploits of Ezra-- a great man of God and a great prayer warrior. Ezra's name literally means "help". Help me Jesus to know you in a more intimate way. Where there is no intimate and personal relationship with God there is no genuine revival. I cry out for your help God. Help me. Assist me. Show me the way, and I will follow Lord Jesus. Help we have fallen and can't get back up. Help me Lord Jesus. Take my hand, help me up and I will rise above my past and present predicaments, problems, and pecarious situations. This helpful real revival revolution begins in the saints hearts individually before it hits the church corporately. Ezra clearly understood the importance of God's help. Recognizing the importance of God's help, he prayed for revival. Dr. Mark Hanby in his book "Anointing The Unsanctified - An Unveiled Revelation In Spiritual Authority, asked a thought-provoking question concerning real revival: "How much do you want a revival? You probably do not want any more than you know you need. Ninety percent of the people do not feel spiritual. They feel God when He moves. They feel the presence of the Lord when they sing. They hear the preacher when he preaches. But we need help in our heads. We need to start thinking 'I must have God.'[2]

39

True revival is the direct result of the fire of the Holy Ghost burning deeply in our hearts. It occurs when we have clearly heard the voice of God concerning a spiritual renewal of His work in our lives. We hear His voice through prayer.

Ezra was a partner with another preacher named Nehemiah. Like Ezra, he was a great man of prayer and God used both Ezra and Nehemiah to be a blessing to the children of Israel.

Stay Committed to God's Work

The Israelites were in exile in Persia. During this time of exile, there were two exoduses from Persia to Jerusalem. The first one was led by a man named Zerubbabel. As the children of Israel left Persia and journeyed to Jerusalem, they wanted to rebuild the Temple, a house for their God, but many enemies came against them. As you will see, they were determined to let nothing dissuade them. Similarly, when you decide to do a work for the Lord, many enemies will come against you, but you must remain committed to that work.

Ezra, realizing that the building of the Temple had not been completed during the first exile, was led of God to organize a second exile from Persia to Jerusalem. His goal was to build the Temple, a house for their God -- the God of Abraham, Isaac and Jacob. The bottom line was that Ezra realized that the house of God is a house of prayer. God wanted to help his people through the passageway of prayer, communication with God, so He could send a real revival revolution in their lives.

Hear the Voice of God

Ezra, as we have already pointed out, was a praying man. He would not take a step without hearing from God. And that's how we must be today, if we want true revival. We must be men and women of prayer. We must clearly hear the voice of our God in order to let the real revival revolution begin in our life.

One night not long ago, the Spirit of the Lord came upon me. I had a burden to pray and to study the Word. The urgency was so great that I stayed up until 4:00 a.m., praying and studying. I had no idea that my father, the late Rev. Dr. Arthur L. Mackey, Sr., the pastor of my local home church which I pastor today would call me that same morning and say, "I want you to come and share the message this morning." By obeying the Spirit of the Lord by burning the midnight oil in prayer God revived my spirit in preparation to minister his word prophetically.

God has His ways of dealing with you, and God has a way of preparing you for things to come. There are some things about the future that I have some knowledge of that I am not free to share publicly, but I know God is about to do many things in our midst. There are some blessings that He has shown me that I can't share at this time because some people would not be ready or able to receive such things.

One thing I can share, however, is that we need to get ready for the blessing that is on the way. We need to get a little reviving. We need to get a little rekindling. We need a time of refreshing from the Lord. George Seary wrote in his song "Revive Us, Lord" that "We need a Holy Ghost revival. Nothing else will do. Nothing but your Spirit, Lord can our hearts renew. As we turn to you and seek your holy face pour out your Spirit in this place." [3]

A Little Space for Grace

Ezra wrote, "And now for a little space grace hath been shewed from the Lord our God..." (Ezra 9:8). This is what we need today -- "A little space for grace."

God knows what is going on in our lives. He knows the messes. He knows the miracles. God knows if we're seeking Him. His Word declares, "Seek ye the Lord while He may be found" (Isa. 55:6). He's not always going to be around for you to be able to seek Him. He's there, but there will come a time when He won't hear what you've got to say. There will be a time when the dispensation of grace will end. There will be a time when He'll crack the eastern sky, and come back for His

Church, returning for His bride, a bride without a spot or a wrinkle.

However, at this time there are many wrinkles in the bridal gown. The dress has to be washed; it has to be cleansed, through the washing of the water of His Word. (See Eph. 5:24) God knows and we know the lies we are living, and the hatred that's in our hearts. We know our own faults, because we have to live with ourselves.

Sometimes I wonder how God can use me, but I remind myself that God understands everything about me. He's able to look beyond our faults and see our needs. There are times when, if we take advantage of the grace of God that is extended to us, He calls us to repentance. That's something that the Church needs to talk more about -- *repentance*.

Some folks say that we don't need to repent, that we don't need to say that we're sorry. Many live according to a humanistic philosophy that says, "Let's just live the way we want to live. Let's just live life to the fullest, and reach our fullest potential and totally forget about repenting of our personal, public, or private sin."

However, in the process they neglect and misuse the Word of God. The Bible shows us that when a nation sins, like Israel sinned against God, the Lord doesn't just call one person to repentance. He calls the entire nation to repentance. That's what we see taking place in Ezra the 9th chapter. God was dealing with Ezra in the time of prayer, because He was calling the children of Israel, the people of God to repentance.

A perpetuating attitude of irresponsibility infects our land today. People don't want to repent. They don't want to say, "Lord, I'm sorry." They fail to see the need to change their lives. They seem unable to see that that's what the gospel message is all about. The Apostle John wrote, "For God so loved the world, that he gave his only begotten Son, that whosoever believeth in him should not perish, but have everlasting life" (John 3:16). Help! We need revival!

We need to be able to say, "Lord, forgive me; I'm wrong." When we admit that we've been wrong about our attitudes, responses, and behaviors, the Lord will bring us out of the difficulties we face. He will restore us. He will revive us, and He will give us a little space of grace. For you cannot worship God in spirit and in truth without a genuine revival of repentance that can only occur by the grace of God.

Nothing Is Too Hard For God

No matter what the problem is, it's not too big for God. God is big enough to deal with all our problems -- if we will let Him. Our arms are too short to box with God. Job, in the midst of his afflictions, was truly down and out. He said, "All the days of my appointed time will I wait [on the Lord] till my change come" (Job 14:14). Job trusted God. He knew that God's timing is always perfect.

The Psalmist wrote, "Though I walk in the midst of trouble, thou wilt revive me: thou shalt stretch forth thine hand against the wrath of mine enemies, and thy right hand shall save me" (Ps. 138:7). This was Job's attitude as well.

Eventually the Lord answered Job in a whirlwind. The answer was in the midst of a storm. In all the hardship, the hell, and the frustration he was going through, there was an answer. The answer was that God was there all the time. In the midst of all of the hell, and all of the frustration, and all of the heartache that we may be facing; it may not seem like God is there, but He is there watching over us. He is the God who is always there.

Sometimes we don't understand the ways of the Lord. At those times we need to listen to the words of the Prophet Isaiah: "For my thoughts are not your thoughts, neither are your ways my ways, saith the Lord. For as the heavens are higher than the earth, so are my ways higher than your ways, and my thoughts than your thoughts" (Isa. 55:8-9). The Key to experiencing real revival in your own situation is to trust God even in the midst of the storm. Job 13:15 declares "Though he slay me, yet will I trust in him: but I will maintain mine own ways before him."

God Raises Up a Remnant

The trusting heart says, "I can't understand what God is doing. If I was Him, I would try to do it another way. But I'm not God, and you're not God. He's in control. He knows what is going on." We might think we're in a mess, but in the midst of the mess God raises up a remnant. A remnant is usually something that you didn't realize was there -- something you had forgotten. There is a remnant of faithful prayer warriors who are seeking the Lord for revival, and their prayers will impact on all our lives. From that remnant, God will raise up someone to encourage you, someone who will help you to be able to escape from the high fire that's about to come. The remnant will help us to escape.

God doesn't want us to perish. He wants us all to be able to receive eternal life. The Bible says, "And He had left us a remnant, and given us a nail in His holy place" (Ezra 9:8).

God has given us a little space of grace -- something to hold on to when we're going through times of confusion and turmoil. The means of escape may be just a nail in His holy place that we're able to reach up and take hold of, because sometimes we can get discouraged even in the household of God. Even if it's just a nail in His holy place that you are able to hold on to, be sure to hold on to that nail. That nail is there as a promise that you've got something to build on. It's something for you to hammer on, something to build with, even though it may be just a little nail. That itsy-bitsy nail is your mighty hope of better things to come. I thank God for the hope of better things to come.

Even though things may not always work out the way we want them to work out, we need to remember the little nail that is there for us in the Holy Place. When I see that little nail, I'm going to pick up my hammer, and I'm going to begin to hammer it on in, in the Name of the Lord. After I hammer that nail in, I will pick up another nail and keep on hammering away. I'll keep on picking up nails and hammering away, and I'll keep on working on the building for my Lord.

Run With the Vision God Gives

Ezra asked God to provide the Israelites with a remnant that would enable them to escape, to give them a nail for the rebuilding of His temple, and to "...lighten our eyes" (Ezra 9:8). Our eyes often become heavy as we journey through this life. At such times, we need divine enlightenment -- the vision of the Lord. There have been many times when we've been up till the wee hours of the morning, fasting, and praying. We want God to lighten our eyes, so that we might see what He wants to do.

In these precious times before His throne, He has shown me things that I can't share, but I know I've seen them. Sometimes I grow concerned by what He shows me and I ask, "Lord, how can that happen if this is at this point, and that's not at that point?"

He will simply answer, *"It's going to come to pass."*

The Word of God declares, "Where there is no vision, the people perish" (Prov. 29:18). Therefore, we must keep our eyes focused on what God shows us. He is showing us how to get to know Him in a more intimate and passionate manner. We need to keep our eyes on Jesus, no matter what's going on around us. We must expect revival to come, not just revival services. We have to speak a word of faith that says, "Lord, let the revival begin in me." We must pray as Ezra did, "...and give us a little reviving in my bondage" (Ezra 9:8). Help! We need revival! Yes Lord, even in our bondage because true freedom consists of spiritual freedom, social freedom, and economic freedom.

In his book, "The Burden of Freedom-Discover the Keys To Your Individual, Community, and National Freedom," Dr. Myles Munroe states that, "True freedom is self-discovery of one's personal purpose and the liberty to pursue the fulfillment of that purpose according to the laws and principles established by God, without restricting others from doing the same."[4]

Stepping Out of Bondage

Ezra wrote, "And now for a little space grace hath been shewed from the Lord our God, to leave us a remnant to escape, and to give us a nail in His holy place, that our God may lighten our eyes, and give us a little reviving in our bondage. For we were bondsmen; yet our God hath not forsaken us in our bondage, but hath extended mercy unto us in the sight of the kings of Persia, to give us a reviving, to set up the house of our God, and to repair the desolation thereof, and to give us a wall in Judah and in Jerusalem" (Ezra 9:8-9).

We need revival in our public and private lives. Revival in our homes. Revival in our churches. God will not forsake us. He will extend His mercy to us and give us a revival so that we can rebuild the house of God and repair all the desolation of our society, our homes, our children, and our schools. A passionate, intamate, and consistant love affair with the Lord of Revival will birth this type of move of the Holy Spirit in the life of the church.

We need to pray as the Psalmist did, "Wilt thou not revive us again: that thy people may rejoice in thee? Shew us thy mercy, O lord, and grant us thy salvation" (Ps. 85:6-7). The Lord will hear our prayer, and He will extend His mercy to us.

Many people may not realize it, but we are like the Israelites were, a people in bondage. Some are shocked by profanity, liquor, pride, money, carnal things, and other forms of idolatry. Whether ours are sins of commission or omission, it's all sin to God. God doesn't see sin like we do -- in measurements of big and little. To Him, it's all sin.

God wants us to experience the fire of revival in our faith, family, and finances; He wants to deliver us from our bondage. God wants to remove from us those things that we don't want to talk about in our testimonies, or that we don't want to talk about when we are in church. Nevertheless, God knows and we know these issues still control us. The Bible says that in our flesh there is no good thing. Yes, we need a little reviving in our homes, for the church, that impacts our community. Let's pray for a heaven-borne revival that will sweep our land so that the people of God will be renewed in the spirit of their mind.

I agree wholeheartedly with Leonard Ravenhill's battle cry for revival as it is expressed in his poem:

LORD, SEND A REVIVAL

I see the peril of the world, I see it rot.
I see the church and know she has not got
What she should have of Calvary love and passion.
She loves her ease and style, and this world's smile and fashion.
O Christ, was it for this that Thou didst bleed?
For churches blind to human need?
For lounging pew warmers who never tell
Of saving grace to sinners bound for hell?

You promised us a baptism of fire.
But here we are, bogged down in slothful mire,
Thy people fat, content, increased in goods,
Resentful if we prod them from their goods,
Forgive them, Father, oh, forgive!
Shake them awake! And let them live
Upon the plane of Pentecostal power---
Less inducement cannot meet this hour.

Before You come to take Your spotless Bride,
We trust You for a world-wide revival tide! [5]

Concerning revival services someone might say, "Oh, it's too much to come out to church every night." The fact is, it is not too much when you look at the bondage that is in your life. You might spend two or three hours in a service, but how much time do you put into that thing that's holding you down from

47

being all God wants you to be? We need a support system. We need to come together. We need to fast. We need to pray. We need to wait on the Lord together, as a people of God. There's so much more involved than simply getting an individual blessing; it's a corporate blessing that will minister to all of us. After all, we're one body in Christ.

What would happen if God were to bless everybody in the house? This will happen if we come together and call on the Name of the Lord. We need to call on Jesus in the midst of our hard times, because God is there to help us and He wants to help us. He was there with Job, and He'll be there with you. He'll bring you through. He'll bring you out. He'll deliver you. He'll restore you. He'll revive you. He'll renew you. He'll change you. He'll revamp you. He will do it, He will do it, He will do it! Yes, He will! He'll do it if you trust Him, if you call on the Name of the Lord, and if you pray, "Lord, I can't make it by myself. I need you to step into our home. I need you to step into my troubled marriage. I need you to step into my relationship. I need you to step into my church. I need you to step into my job. I need you to step into my finances. I need you to step into my troubled mind. I need you to step into my wounded spirit. I've been down too long, and I feel like I can't get up."

Redeem the Time for the Days Are Evil

Through the voice of the Prophet Isaiah God declared: "For thus saith the high and lofty One that inhabiteth eternity, whose name is Holy; I dwell in the high and holy place, with him also that is of a contrite and humble spirit, to revive the spirit of the humble, and to revive the heart of the contrite ones" (Isa. 57:15). God will revive the believer who is crushed to the point that He will heed God's call to repentence and obey His will. A humble spirit says God's way is right and I am wrong. Therefore I am going to do things Your way Lord.

Contrition and humility, along with prayer and repentance, are keys to revival. God says, "If my people, which are called by my name, shall humble themselves, and pray, and seek my face, and turn from their wicked ways; then will I hear from heaven, and will forgive their sin, and will heal their land" (2 Chron. 7:14). God is calling us to humble ourselves in His presence and to turn from our wicked ways.

This is what the Lord means when He says, "Let the weak say I am strong." I am weak sometimes, I'm down sometimes, but He makes me strong. I'm poor sometimes, and it seems as if I don't have the money to make ends meet, but He makes a way, He opens a door that no man can close. We need to remember what He has done for us and to believe that He will always be faithful to us. What we really need is to get revived. We need to pray, "Lord, we need revival." Then we can walk confidently through the door to revival that God opens up, because we know Jesus is coming back. Yes, He's coming back, He's coming back. "Even so, come quickly, Lord Jesus" (Rev. 22:20).

Jesus promised His disciples, "In three days will I rise again." The Bible also tells us that "a thousand years is as one day with the Lord." The year 2001 marked the beginning of the third "day" -- the third millennium of human history, since the life, death and resurrection of Jesus Christ. I don't know if He's coming back on that day, but I do know that He will be returning soon, and very soon.

Look at the signs of the times. All you have to do is to turn on cablevision and you will see women kissing women, and men holding men. We are living in times worse than Sodom and Gomorrah. When you go into New York City, you see all types of things in the city that never sleeps. This is true of all the major cities of the world as well.

God says that judgment must begin in the household of God. We must let the judgment come. We must let God's holy fire burn away all the dross. I believe it is appropriate to pray, "Burn me, Lord" and "Cleanse me, Lord." Let us pray with all sincerity, "Get me right, Lord, for a job--for the job you have for me to do."

Leonard Ravenhill's poem, "THE REVIVAL SONG," powerfully drives home the reality of our dire need for true revival:

> Lord, we are hungry for blessing,
> This is in tune with Thy Word;
> Now as our need we're confessing,
> Give us new hearts, cleansed and stirred.
>
> Great is the need of our nations,
> Great is the need of this hour.
> Lord, we abhor our stagnation,
> Answer with Holy Ghost power.
>
> Look on our great desperation;
> Hold back Thy judgement we pray.
> Move through the length of our nation;
> Open Thy windows today.
>
> Lord, fill the Church with Thy Spirit.
> Lord, save our nation, we pray.
> Quicken our love and our zeal, and
> Send us *revival* today! [6]

Stop Sleeping with the Enemy

We have to stop sleeping with the enemy. Ezra 9: brings home this point quite clearly, for as Ezra was praying and calling for God to send a time of reviving, he realized that the sons of Israel were sleeping with and marrying the daughters of pagan religions. Because of this, God could not use His people. Their immorality would bring a curse upon generations yet to be born. Therefore, He had to use Ezra to call the people to repentance. The people of God were sleeping in the enemy's camp.

Like the Israelites of old, there are many who are sleeping in the enemy's camp today. These are people who are not praying, not fasting--and those who come to church just for a social scene. We need a move of God. We need to be serious about what God can do in our community. We can't have a humanistic philosophy or any other philosophy. We must believe every word of the Bible. When the Word of God says, "For we were bondsmen; yet our God hath not forsaken us in our bondage" (Ezra 9:9), we must believe it.

Even though God knew they were sleeping with the enemy, He did not forsake them. He sent a prophet to warn them. God is not finished with us. There is something in you, and there is something in me that God can still use. In spite of all of our faults, in spite of the fact that we may have missed God several times, there is still something that a Sunday school teacher told us that we can hold on to. There is still something that we heard some preacher say that we can cling to. There is still something that we received when a song of Zion was sung, that can change our lives, including our attitudes.

William P. Mackay's classic hymn, "Revive Us Again," truly summarizes the message of this chapter.

> We praise Thee, O God, for the Son of Thy Love,
> For Jesus who died and is now gone above.
> We praise Thee, O God, for Thy Spirit of light,
> Who has shown us our Savior and scattered our night.
> All glory and praise to the Lamb that was slain,
> Who has borne all our sins and has cleansed every stain.
> Revive us again; fill each heart with Thy love,
> May each soul be rekindled with fire from above.
> Hallelujah, Thine the glory! Hallelujah, Amen!
> Hallelujah, Thine the glory! Revive us again!

God is going to send revival. [7]

Yes, God is sending real revival daily and many of the drug dealers in the inner city, the suburbs, and rural areas will give their life to Christ and be Deacons, Preachers, Teachers, Bishops and Willing Workers for Christ, who will be radical

Arthur L. Mackey, Jr.

revolutionaries representing the Lord of Real Revival. Receive your Personal revival my brother and my sister put down your crack and your other drugs, and get high on the life changing power of the lover of your soul, Jesus Christ!!! Get ready for your personal real revival revolution!!!

Chapter 2

SEEKING GOD -- THE FOUNDATION OF REAL REVIVAL

Put First Things First

"Moreover when ye fast, be not, as the hypocrites, of a sad countenance: for they disfigure their faces, that they may appear unto men to fast. Verily I say unto you, they have their reward."

"But thou, when thou fastest, anoint thine head, and wash thy face; That thou appear not unto men to fast, but unto thy Father which is in secret: and thy Father, which seeth in secret, shall reward thee openly."

"Lay not up for yourselves treasures upon earth, where moth nor rust doth corrupt, and where thieves do not break through nor steal:"

"For where your treasure is, there will your heart be also."

"The light of the body is the eye: if therefore thine eye be single, thy whole body shall be full of light."

"But if thine eye be evil, thy whole body shall be full of darkness. If therefore the light that is in thee be darkness, how great is that darkness!"

"No man can serve two masters: for either he will hate the one, and love the other; or else he will hold to the one, and despise the other. Ye cannot serve God and mammon."

"Therefore I say unto you, Take not thought for your life, what ye shall eat, or what ye shall drink; nor yet for your body, what ye shall put on. Is not the life more than meat, and the body than raiment?"

"Behold the fowls of the air; for they sow not, neither do they reap, nor gather into barns; yet your heavenly Father feedeth them. Are ye not much better than they?"

"Which of you by taking thought can add one cubit unto his stature?"

"And why take ye thought for raiment? Consider the lilies of the field, how they grow; they toil not, neither do they spin:"

"And yet I say unto you, That even Solomon in all his glory was not arrayed like one of these."

"Wherefore, if God so clothed the grass of the field, which today is, and tomorrow is cast into the oven, shall he not much more clothe you, O ye of little faith?"

"Therefore take no thought, saying, What shall we eat? or, What shall we drink? or, Wherewithal shall we be clothed?"

"(For after all these things do the Gentiles seek:) for your heavenly Father knoweth that ye have need of all these things."

"But seek ye first the kingdom of God, and his righteousness; and all these things shall be added unto you."

"Take therefore no thought for the morrow: for the morrow shall take thought for the things of itself. Sufficient unto the day is the evil thereof" (Matt. 6:16-34).

The focus of this chapter is on Matthew 6:33, "Seek ye first the kingdom of God, and his righteousness; and all these things shall be added unto you."

We need to seek God in the midst of the pain, and in the midst of turmoil. We need to seek God in the good times, and also seek Him in the bad times. Always remember that seeking the face and not the hand of God is the foundation of revival. Real revival is never ever birthed through seeking a mere revival meeting, real revival is only birthed through believers who desperately seek the face of God daily without ceasing in prayer.

Seek the Lord

Job, in the midst of great suffering, knew this, and he said, "I would seek unto God, and unto God would I commit my cause" (Job 5:8).

When everything is going well it seems easy to go to church, and to say, "I'm going to church to praise the Lord." But when you're going through hard times, when you're going through the hell fire, when everything seems to be going wrong, that is the time to press forward, and to earnestly seek the face of God.

The Psalmist knew this truth when he wrote: "When thou saidst, Seek ye my face; my heart said unto thee, Thy face, Lord, will I seek" (Ps. 27:8).

That seeking brings God's blessing is an age-old truth. The writer of 2nd Chronicles prophesies in behalf of the Lord: "If my people, which are called by my name, shall humble themselves, and pray, and seek *my face*, and turn from their wicked ways; then will I hear from heaven, and will forgive their sin, and I will heal their land" (2 Chron. 7:14, italics mine). Oh, we need healing in the land, we need healing in our schools, we need healing in our homes, our hearts, our churches, and our world. That heaven-borne healing begins with humility, prayer, and seeking the face of the Lord. Seek the Reviver, Jesus Christ, and not the revival. Seek the Blessor, and not the blessing. Seek the Healer, and not the healing.

The Prophet Daniel knew how important this is when he wrote, " I set my face unto the Lord God, to seek by prayer and supplications, with fasting, and sackcloth, and ashes" (Dan. 9:3). Seeking the face of God takes us out of selfish motives and brings us into the pressence God to deal with our pain and learn how to overcome.

As Isaiah pointed out, our ways are not God's ways, and our thoughts are not God's thoughts. "For as the heavens are higher than the earth, so are my ways higher than your ways, and my thoughts than your thoughts" (Isa. 55:9).

55

God sees the total picture, and He has a mind that is able to look at a particular situation and say, "This is the way to solve it," but we'll never know His perfect answer unless we seek His face and get down on our knees before Him. Like Hezekiah, we need to turn our face to the wall and say, "It's me, it's me, it's me, O Lord, standing in the need of prayer. It's not my mother, it's not my farther, but it's me, O Lord, standing in the need of prayer."

Trust in the Lord

"And they that know thy name will put their trust in thee: for thou, Lord, hath not forsaken them that seek thee" (Ps. 9:10). We need to get on our knees and say, "I trust in you, Lord, with all my heart. Instead of leaning unto my own understanding, I will acknowledge you in all my ways." (See Prov. 3:5-6)

Jesus said, "Without me ye can do nothing" (John 15:5). We need to remember that we can't do what God wants us to do on our own. We can't do it in our own might. We can't trust in our own ability, because we've got to depend upon the ability of God. God is able to accomplish all things; the only thing He cannot do is fail.

Paul wrote, "Now unto him that is able to do exceeding abundantly above all that we ask or think, according to the power that worketh in us" (Eph. 3:20). We need to remember that God is always able.

Jesus gave us the key when He said, "Seek ye first the kingdom of God" (Matt. 6:33). When we look into the New Testament Greek, we get a clearer meaning of this verse from the Sermon on the Mount. Some of the most powerful statements Jesus ever made are found in this particular passage. Jesus told the assembled throng not to try to serve both God and mammon, because a person cannot have two masters. (See Matt. 6:24.) He also pointed out that a person can't serve both God and money, because He knew, as Paul later pointed out, that the love of money is the root of all evil. (See 1 Tim. 6:10.)

Money is not the root of all evil. It is a medium that we need. Money, in and of itself, is neither good nor evil, but when an evil person uses money for evil purposes, then it becomes evil. It is the love of money -- idolizing it -- that the Bible condemns. If a good person gets money and says, "I want to use it for building the Kingdom of God, I want to use it so the preaching of God's Word can go across the airways, so the preaching of God's Word can be printed, so churches can be built, so the Gospel can go forth in a mighty way and be spread throughout the nations," then evil money becomes good money.

Where Is Your Treasure?

The Bible says that money is able to answer good things and bad things. The key to which answer it gives depends on where your heart is. Jesus said, "Where your treasure is, there will your heart be also" (Matt. 6:21). If you're a corrupt person, your money is going to be corrupt right along with you. If you're thinking evil thoughts, then your money will be spent on the pursuit of evil. For example, if pornography is of interest to you, you will spend your money on pornographic magazines and videos. If you have a problem with alcohol, you will spend your money at the bar or the liquor store.

The way we spend our money shows where we are spiritually, but if we have a heart that is right with God, His Spirit will convict us concerning how we use our money, and He will tell us how much money and when we are to give to the work of the ministry. He will provide what we need to support our family and to pay our bills. He'll also show us how to let money be an example and a living witness for our Lord Jesus Christ.

The King James Version says, "Seek ye first the kingdom of God, and his righteousness." The Kingdom of God and His righteousness are inextricably joined together. Paul wrote, "For the kingdom of God is not meat and drink; but righteousness, and peace, and joy in the Holy Ghost" (Rom. 14:17).

Arthur L. Mackey, Jr.

You simply cannot have the Kingdom of God without righteousness. If you're not in a right-standing relationship with the Lord, then you cannot be in the Kingdom of God. By righteousness I mean a right-standing relationship with the Lord. In many respects, this is like any good relationship, whether it's a relationship with a spouse or a sweetheart. You need to be in right standing with the other person in order to have a good relationship. When our heart is right with God, our relationship with Him is right and the result is righteousness.

Royal-Born Members of the Kingdom of God

"Jesus answered and said unto him, Verily, verily, I say unto thee, Except a man be born again, he cannot see the kingdom of God" (John 3:3). If you're not born again, if you haven't been baptized in His blood, if you haven't been crucified in Him, then you cannot partake of the Kingdom of God.

The Bible says, "If thou shalt confess with thy mouth the Lord Jesus, and shalt believe in thine heart that God hath raised him from the dead, thou shalt be saved" (Rom. 10:9). You might still have some problems, hardships and difficulties that you're going through. You may feel that certain things are holding you back, but if you confess with your mouth, and believe in your heart that He's risen from the dead, God will take you into His kingdom. He declares, *Everything else that seems to be a problem, I'll work it out, I'll work it out to be a testimony.* Bishop Philip H. Porter, Jr., states, "We have no good reason to pursue emptiness, shallow success, or a hollow career. Jesus Christ can guide us on a path that makes life worth living. And He will walk along that pathway with us. I have committed my life to staying on the path to purity. That path of purity is the only viable course in a fallen world that is out of control."[1]

Keep on Seeking

Seek God and His kingdom. The Bible says, "Seek ye the Lord while he may be found, call ye upon him while he is near"

(Isa. 55:6). I've got news for you: we are in the dispensation of grace right now, and the Lord is among us. He's opened up doors for us that no man can close. He has said, "Behold, I set before you an open door, and no man can close it." We have opportunity upon opportunity right in front of us in the here-and-now.

Christian book stores carry all sorts of Bible versions. You can find a King James version, the New International version, a version for the children, the Bible on computer, the Bible on disk, and all sorts of other versions and different translations. The World of God is all over the place, and we have multitudinous opportunities to witness on our job, in our home, in the supermarket -- everywhere we go.

While There Is Time

We are living in the last days. Jesus could come back at any moment. This is why it's so important for us to take advantage of all the opportunities we currently have -- "Redeeming the time, because the days are evil" (Eph. 5:16).

The time we have left to build the Kingdom of God is short. The signs of the times show us how close we are to the end.

We're living in a time of great technological advances as well. Sheep are being cloned, babies are developed in test tubes and scientists keep trying to play God. What was once science fiction has become reality. People are even thinking of the possibility of cloning human beings through genetic engineering and the manipulation of DNA.

How easily mankind forgets that there is only one Creator, only one true God. He is the one who should get all the glory, all the honor, and all the praise. We need to seek Him while He may be found -- before the time of the Great Tribulation, before the mark of the beast is forced upon people, before the time in which the number 666 will be spread throughout the land, before the Rapture of the Church. We must seek the Lord while He may be found, because our Master is coming back.

Seeking and Worship As One

The Greek word for "seek" is *zeteo*. It means more than simply to seek. It also means to worship. When we seek God, we worship Him. Everyone worships someone or something. For example, some may worship their new car and then will go out everyday and wash that car, polish that car, shine the chrome and put special polish on the wheels. These folks truly love their car, they worship their car.

Some men worship beautiful women. Every time they see a beautiful woman they just shake their heads. Some women worship handsome, strong men. Others worship fame, fortune, or fun. Intellectuals may worship study and education. Truly, everyone worships something.

But God is calling us to worship Him.

Worship in Spirit and in Truth

Jesus said, "But the hour cometh, and now is, when the true worshippers shall worship the Father in spirit and in truth: for the Father seeketh such to worship Him. God is a Spirit: and they that worship Him must worship Him in spirit and in truth" (John 4:23-24).

To seek means to worship. It also means to plot. Some people are in the church not because they want to be a part of the Kingdom of God, but because they want to set-up their own kingdom. In this case they're "plotting," not seeking God and His kingdom, and they're involved in selfish planning. In the process they're doing their own thing against the life and the blessings of God.

These people are self-seekers, but God wants us to seek Him. We've got to be seriously involved in this business. God is seeking for true worshipers, and true worshipers should be seeking Him and His righteousness.

"They should seek the Lord, if haply they might feel after Him, and find Him, though he be not far from every one of us:

For in Him we live, and move, and have our being" (Act 17 & 28). God wants us to seek Him and to reach out for Him so that we will find Him. He is never far from any of us.

The Bible says, "Draw nigh to God, and He will draw nigh to you" (James 4:8).

A Burning Desire to Serve the Lord

The Prophet Jeremiah wrote, "Ye shall seek me, and find me, when ye shall search for me with all your heart" (Jer. 29:13). Searching for the Lord with all our heart creates a burning desire to service Him.

To know the Lord intimately, we must always be endeavoring to get closer to Him, to reach out for holiness, to inquire more and more about how we can learn about the things of God. It doesn't matter whether you've been in the church for fifty years, seventy-five years, one hundred years or more. There is always more that each of us can learn about the move of God. If we knew everything about God we would die instantly.

Every time I hear a preacher preach, every time I hear a deacon or a trustee pray, a choir sing, or a member of a congregation share a testimony, there's a little bit more that I understand about Jesus.

What are we seeking? Are we truly seeking the Kingdom of God? There are many kingdoms in the world and within the Church. There is the kingdom of self, the kingdom of politics, religious kingdoms, business kingdoms, and many others. Many of the disciples and followers of Jesus thought He would set up a political, earthly kingdom. But the Kingdom of God is not political. The Kingdom of God is a kingdom of righteousness, peace, and joy in the Holy Spirit. Jesus said, "Seek ye first the kingdom of God and His righteousness." This means that in order to have the kingdom, we need to have a right relationship with the Lord. That kind of righteous kingdom relationship involves hearing from Him, listening for His voice, and understanding His Word. I am reminded of the saying written by

Howard Springer: "The kingdom of God is not going to be advanced by our churches becoming filled with men, but by men in our churches becoming filled with God."[2]

The Royalty, the Rule and the Realm of God

The Kingdom of God exists wherever the King rules and reigns. The Kingdom literally means the royalty, the rule or the realm of God. Jesus is more than our Savoir; He wants to be our Lord and King. We've got to move into being a part of the Kingdom, based upon His royalty, His rule in His realm.

We have to ask, Who's the boss? God wants to be your Lord. Are you His slave? I'm proud to be able to say, "I'm seeking and I'm striving to be a slave of the Lord, to be His property."

The Kingdom and the rule of God are not political. God is not a Democrat, an Independent, or a Republican. "God is a Spirit, and they that worship Him, must worship Him in spirit and in truth." The winds that are blowing during this current political time are very dangerous, because there is so much division and people are becoming polarized from each other.

In times like these it is important to remember that even though the answer to the problems in our society are not political, the Kingdom of God can have a great political impact. Take a look at how God used David and Nehemiah to effect social changes in the world and see how the power of God and the Kingdom of God can cause society to change. Even so, the Kingdom of God is not political; it is a move of God. We must be careful not to confuse the two realms. What the kingdom of this world needs is a move of God's Spirit. The Kingdom of God is in our hearts. It is not political; it is spiritual, so we have to seek God and His kingdom in spirit and in truth.

Seeking God Imparts Life

"Seek ye me, and ye shall live" (Amos 5:4). This is what the Lord says to the house of Israel: "Seek the Lord, and ye shall live" (Amos 5:6).

God has blessed His church. The Church of Jesus Christ is much more than stained glass windows, lush carpeting, comfortable pews and other building improvements. The Church of Jesus Christ is His people. He would like to impart life to His people. The Lord says that if we will seek Him, He will impart life to us.

In Times of Drought Our Roots Grow Deeper

"O God, thou art my God; early will I seek thee: my soul thirsteth for thee, my flesh longeth for thee in a dry and thirsty land, where no water is" (Ps. 63:1). The effect of dry times is to cause us to seek. In times of drought, the roots of plants go deeper in search of life-giving water. The Psalmist shows us that the spiritual life is the same. "O God, thou art my God, early will I seek thee: my soul thirsteth for thee, my flesh longeth for thee in a dry and weary land, where no water is."

Our responsibility is to seek God, and He will take care of our thirst.

We have to seek the Kingdom of God, but we must also seek His righteousness. The Greek word for righteousness is *dikaios* which means "equity of character." Equity, as you know, is something of value that continues to grow, as in the case of real estate. God's righteousness continues to build within our characters. There's a big difference between being God-righteous and self-righteous. God hates the philosophy of me, myself and I. God hates self-righteousness and He hates the attitude of "holier than thou," because God says, "Be ye holy, because I am holy."

God's righteousness is equity of character, which means that He is not only concerned about your calling, whether you've been called to be a preacher, a teacher, a prophet, an evangelist, a

63

deacon, a trustee, a church member, or a choir member. Yes, the gifts and callings of God come without repentance, and that's why I sometimes see people get up and prophecy, and they lay hands on people, but they don't live a life that's worth anything. In spite of this, once God calls you, He seals you. He will not take that calling back.

A Character Strong in Righteousness

We've really got to take a careful look at our character. The true test of character involves our choices when nobody else is around. It is, as someone has pointed out, what we do in the dark. This really tells the world who we are, as they observe how we behave when other believers do not see us. This aspect of character goes beyond preaching from the pulpit, singing in the choir, taking the offering, or standing up in the congregation and lifting our hands. But what do we do in the midnight hour when nobody else is looking? That's when righteousness really comes into play. A great overwhelming appreciation that Jesus made me righteous by shedding his blood for me.

We become righteous through justification by faith. "Justification" means "just as if I've never sinned." Despite my sins and failings, in God's eyes. His blood covers me. It covers all of my thoughts, all of my messes, all of my hang-ups. All of my "hook-ups" are taken care of through His justification and righteousness. He has called me into a right-standing relationship with Him, and this gives me some equity, something to fall back on when temptation comes. We can overcome by the blood of the Lamb and the word of our testimony. I get some spiritual support that can back me up, some equity. In difficult times, this equity gives me something to fall back on. In other words I am righteous only because of the finished work of Christ on the cross, and not because of anything I have done. You will experience real revival when you embrace the truth that you are righteous because you are covered by the blood of Jesus Christ.

God's Promise to Seekers

The promise is, "Seek ye first the kingdom of God and His righteousness," and then, all these things will be added unto you". (See Matt. 6:33)

When I began to seek God, I didn't have to go around asking people for anything. I simply began to seek God, and people started to get in touch with me. God, in His wisdom and in His perfect way, began to open doors for me.

If you seek the Lord while He may be found, there are some things that He will simply "add unto you." He will take care of many of the problems you worry about. How I thank God that He adds things to us. He gives us so many things. However, we have to remember that there are some things that He'll subtract from us if we don't seek His face. Sometimes, though, He will multiply many things to those who seek Him. On the other hand, if we don't seek His face, there are some things that He will divide. God wants to add many things to your life, and He only gives one prerequisite: Seek God and His righteousness.

When we seek the Kingdom of God and the face of God He adorns us with blessings. Even though we can't see them, there are blessings upon the horizon as well. There in the distance, God has already prepared them. He just wants us to seek His face, so He can release them. God wants to release blessings to us, but He first wants to know, "Can I trust you with these blessings? If I bless you financially, are you going to spend them on liquor? Are you going to spend it on wine? Are you going to spend it on different women and/or different guys on the dance floor? If I bless you with the finances, will you use it to uplift My kingdom?" When God can trust you He will manifest blessings that He prepared for us before the foundations of the earth was layed. When you do the right thing with fifty cents. Then God can trust you with fifty dollars. When he can trust you with fifty dollars then He can try you with five hundred. God wants you to pass the test of finances so he can manifest the blessing in your life.

65

Arthur L. Mackey, Jr.

There is a season that God has set aside for each one of us. He wants us to prosper with His blessing. Your season may not be my season and my season may not be your season. There are some individual seasons, but there's a corporate season of God's blessings as well. If we seek Him as a church and as a community, there is a corporate blessing God will ordain that is far greater than any legislative law.

There is a corporate blessing that the President cannot pass down. Only God can do it. We've got to seek the face of God.

The Kingdom of God Is Within Us

The kingdom of God is in our hearts. Jesus said, "The kingdom of God is within you" (Luke 17:21). In a similar vein, Paul wrote, "For the kingdom of God is not in word but power" (1 Cor. 4:20).

Too many of us have been trying to do it our way for too long. But if you seek God while He may be found, He will turn it around and add a blessing. Do you need a blessing that needs to be added to your life? Seek God and He'll bless you, He'll bring you through, He'll open up doors that no man can close. He will do it if you trust Him.

Rape victim God wants to touch you right now with a personal revival in your wounded soul and give you victory. Trust in the Lord of Revival, Jesus Christ, He wants to make you whole again through the vehicle of prayer – the fuel of real revival.

You are not alone in your pain. God is right here with you to bring you through the worst tradgedies of life. Whether you have been raped physically, mentally, or spiritually. God will give you the victory.

Chapter 3

PRAYER -- THE FUEL OF REAL REVIVAL

The Power of Praise and Worship

One writer said that we don't need a political uprising, we just need a word from the Lord. Just one word from the Lord will calm all of the doubts and cease all of the fears within our lives. Several years ago, God gave me just one word. He simply said, *"Praise."* And then after He gave me that word, He said, *"Praise Me."* And that whole year in my ministry, I just emphasized worship and praise. I specifically emphasized praise, and began praising God for the things He has accomplished in my life.

I learned to praise God and to discover what praise is all about. I learned to open my mouth, and to thank Him for His goodness, to thank Him for His mercy, to thank Him for His kindness and grace. There are many things God does in our lives that He doesn't have to do. We need to learn not to take these things for granted and to learn to appreciate our church families, our pastors and other church leaders because "we have not many fathers," the Bible points out. We need to remember to thank God for our pastors who have the heart of a shepherd and the heart of a father. They steer us in the right direction.

God laid it on my heart to praise Him for all of these things. And then God gave me another word. He simply said, *"Worship."* This rhema word from God moved me to the next level. Praise is good, to be sure, but God also wanted me to understand worship. Worship is vitally important in our lives. There are times when it seems as if God is not there when we are going through a Job-like experience. At times we almost want to curse God and die. We go through many afflictions and many hard times. We struggle with trying to find the presence of the Lord in our particular situation.

In those kinds of circumstances and times God began to deal with me. He gave me a word, *"Worship."* I began to learn to worship Him because of who He is, simply because He is God. He is in control of the circumstances. He's in charge of this universe. Learning to worship the Lord led me to understand, "The earth is the Lord's, and the fullness thereof; the world, and they that dwell therein" (Ps. 24:1). He was calling me to worship Him.

Praise, Then Worship, Then Prayer

Then, in my own prayer life, God began to deal with me. He gave me the word *"Prayer."*

"And I set my face unto the Lord God, to seek by prayer and supplications, with fasting, and sackcloth, and ashes: And I prayed unto the Lord my God, and made my confession. I said, O Lord, the great and dreadful God, keeping the covenant and mercy to them that love him, and to them that keep his commandments" (Dan. 9:4). So I turned to the Lord God and pleaded with Him in prayer and petition, in fasting, and in sackcloth and ashes.

Before He could deal with me about prayer, the Lord had to teach me about praise personally. Then He had to teach me about worship. When I had attained a somewhat limited understanding of praise and worship, I was able to begin to delve into the meaning and power of prayer. These are the personal words God has given to me, and these are words for the entire Body of Christ as well.

Our Destiny in God

God wants us to become more of a church family so that we can do the things He wants us to do. In this way we will be able to fulfill our destiny as the people of God. God has ordained a destiny for us. The things He has ordained will come to pass if we will cooperate with Him in the fulfillment of His plan.

He has both a personal destiny and a corporate destiny for us -- His family. He has a plan for our lives both individually and collectively. My prayer is, "Lord, I want to cooperate with you in the fulfillment of the plan that you have for my life." I want to help Him fulfill that plan in my home, in my family and in the church.

These are essential ingredients in God's plan for revival. He wants us to learn to praise Him in all things, to pray without ceasing, and to worship Him in spirit and in truth. He wants us to do these things at home, in church, in the marketplace and in our places of business as well.

Revive Us Again

Always remember that prayer is the fuel of revival. Prayer is the gasoline that runs your spiritual engine. True revival is impossible without effective prayer.

The Bible says, "Wilt thou not revive us again: that thy people may rejoice in thee?" (Ps. 85:6).

The Psalmist's prayer is a direct request to our Father in heaven. Notice that one direct result of revival is the ability to rejoice in the Lord.

The Power of Prayer

"And it came to pass, that as he was praying in a certain place, when he ceased, one of his disciples said unto him, Lord, teach us to pray, as John also taught his disciples. And he said unto them, When ye pray, say, Our Father which art in heaven, Hallowed be thy name. Thy kingdom come. Thy will be done, as in heaven, so in earth. Give us day by day our daily bread. And forgive us our sins; for we also forgive everyone who is indebted to us. And lead us not into temptation but deliver us from evil. For thine is the kingdom and the power and the glory forever.

"And he said unto them, which of you shall have a friend, and shall go unto him at midnight, and say unto him, Friend, lend me three loaves; for a friend of mine in his journey is come to me, and I have nothing to set before him. And he from within shall answer and say, Trouble me not: the door is now shut, and my children are with me in bed; I cannot rise and give thee.

"I say unto you, Though he will not rise and give him, because he is his friend, yet because of his importunity he will rise and give him as much as he needs. And I say unto you, Ask, and it shall be given you: seek, and ye shall find; knock, and it shall be opened unto you. For every one that asketh receiveth: and he that seeketh findeth: and to him that knocketh it shall be opened. If a son shall ask bread of any of you that is a father, will he give him a stone? or if he ask a fish, will he for a fish give him a serpent? Or if he shall ask an egg, will he offer him a scorpion? If ye then, being evil, know how to give good gifts unto your children: how much more shall your heavenly Father give the Holy Spirit to them that ask?" (Luke 11:1-13).

The disciples came to Jesus and asked Him to teach them how to pray: "Lord, teach us to pray, as John taught also his disciples." They were speaking of Jesus' cousin, John the Baptist, who was a praying man. He had been out in the wilderness crying out for people to prepare the way of the Lord. His food was locusts, out there in the woods. He didn't get a chance to hear the great preachers of the day. He didn't get a chance to watch Christian television programs, and listen to the best of gospel music, or to find out who was on the "Top 40" gospel chart. But he did know about getting out in the woods and calling on the name of the Lord. John the Baptist positively influenced the disciples of Jesus when they saw his witness, his prayer life and his devotion. Campus Crusade for Christ International President Bill Bright states that, "one prelude to the current revival movement has been the accelerated and unprecedented movement of prayers world-wide. God is hearing the prayers of millions of His children around the world. Revival begins with prayer and results in evangelism."[1]

The Model Prayer of Jesus

Most of us know the prayer that Jesus taught to His disciples as the Lord's Prayer, but in reality it is a model prayer, an outline Jesus gave to His disciples for purposes of instruction in prayer. This isn't the prayer that Jesus prayed when He was in the Garden of Gethsemene, and it isn't the prayer He used when He cried out to His Father in times of temptation and unrest. This is the model prayer He gave for us to use in our own prayer lives.

He's telling us that if we want to know about prayer, we should pattern our prayers after His example. He's also saying, in essence, that this is the type of prayer that will get results. It is a prayer that might mess up some of your plans and programs, and it may play havoc with your agenda. But if you're serious about prayer, if you're serious about communication with God, Jesus has given us the perfect example in His model prayer.

Prayer is a dialogue between two individuals -- the individual who is praying (the servant of God), and God himself. He does not just hear prayer, but He also answers prayer. Many times we use prayer to ask God to give us certain things, but we don't always want His answer, because His answer may not be the thing we desire. I agree with the quote by Leonard Ravenhill, *Revival Praying* (Bethany House Publishers, Minneapolis, Minnesota, 1962, 1996): "Revival can be brought to this generation by prayer, by faith, by cleansing and by obedience to the will of God."[2]

God's Timing Is Perfect

Many times God will answer our prayers with, "*Yes*". But there are other times when He will say, "*Wait a little while; it's not My time yet.*" God's timing is perfect.

God called the Apostle Paul, but yet there was a time of separation after He struck him down from his horse. In fact, there was a period of some thirteen years before Paul really began to go forth in the fullness of his ministry. Why? Because God had to perfect his character. God had to work on the inside of him, and get him prepared to write one-third of the New Testament. In God's perfect timing, Paul was being prepared to become the leader He called him to be.

God wants to take us through a season of preparation as well. God wants to put His character into us. We can have a great calling from the Lord, but He wants change in our character, He wants to deal with us. He will not do things our way, but He wants us to learn to do things His way.

God is Our Father

In essence, Jesus is saying to His disciples, "Let me teach you about prayer, because it is the fuel of revival." He says, "When you pray, say, *Our Father*." First of all, He wants them to know that God is masculine; He is a father. This is very important information because God is a Father to the fatherless. This fact is important for every boy, girl and woman to know. God, in His vast foreknowledge, realized that there would be an absence of fathers in the home.

God knew that in many cases, there would not be a strong male presence in many homes and families. This is why each of us need to stand upon the strong foundation that God is our Father, even if there is no daddy in the home. When a fatherless child is connected to the knowledge that God is his or her Father, that child can succeed.

Certain statistics say that if a father is not in the home, the children in that home have a higher likelihood of going to prison or ending up in trouble. But our Father-God is stronger than statistics. He is stronger than anything that newspapers can report. The reason why our young men and young women will be able to make it is because of the Father.

Jesus declares, *"I want you to start your prayer life correctly; I want you to pray to the Father."* Later on, the

Scriptures tell us to call on the Father in the name of Jesus. But the Master didn't tell them that right away, because He had to prepare them for that. Therefore, He just told them, "I want you to say, *Our Father, which art in heaven, hallowed be Thy name.*"

The Holiest of All Names

Through His model prayer, Jesus teaches His disciples, "*I want you to enter into worship and praise. I want you to realize that the name of the Lord is Holy; He is the Creator of the universe, and hallowed, or "Holy", is His name.*"

We know it's only because of God that we can even get into heaven. All of our righteousness is like filthy rags in His sight. But through the blood of Jesus, the Word says, "It's not by might, nor by power, but by My Spirit, saith the Lord." It's only because of what God has done that we can even be used by Him.

Let God's Kingdom Come

Next, in His model prayer, Jesus says, "Thy kingdom come."

When we get serious about prayer, realizing that it is the fuel of revival, God begins to mess up our plans and program. When we get serious about prayer, God begins to mess up our agenda.

"O Lord, I have heard thy speech, and was afraid: O Lord, revive thy work in the midst of the years, in the midst of the years make known; in wrath remember mercy" (Hab. 3:2). This is a prophet's prayer for revival.

When we get serious about prayer for revival, God will tell us to throw our plans away and to replace them with His plans. He will tell us to throw our ideas away. It's not good ideas that we need; we need some God ideas.

We need to hear the voice of the Lord speaking to us. Moses didn't pop up with his own idea and say, "Let my people go." That wasn't his idea, but the Spirit of the Lord spoke to him in the form of a burning bush. We need the Lord to bring us some burning bushes, and to start burning our bridges behind us.

Arthur L. Mackey, Jr.

We need to hear from God so our concepts can be thrown aside, and we can re-evaluate how we do things, even though they've been done in certain ways for so many years. The cry of our hearts should be, "What does God have to say about the situation?"

Jesus tells His disciples, "If you want to be serious about prayer, the fuel of revival, then you've got to throw away your little kingdoms. You've got to throw away your little cliques and ask God's kingdom to come." Preachers have their cliques, and some have built kingdoms unto themselves. Likewise, some church members have cliques and kingdoms unto themselves. For example, folks who want to sleep around with other church members will get together. Each group becomes a clique that is built around a particular form of sin. But Jesus reminds us that the appropriate prayer is "Thy kingdom come." All other kingdoms will fall under the power of God's kingdom.

When Jesus went out to preach, He didn't preach just about himself. Instead, He called for people to repent, "...for the kingdom of heaven is at hand." He wanted to lift up the Holy name of His Father. This was true even when He said, "If I be lifted up, all men will be drawn unto Me." He knew that this would happen because of His Father in heaven.

Jesus was interested in doing the will of His Father. He wasn't out there doing His own thing. Therefore, He says, "Thy kingdom come, thy plan come, thy agenda come, Thy will be done on earth as it is in heaven." In other words, God had a whole book on our lives. We need to go to Him in prayer, and to find out what He has written about us. That's the only way. It's the only way that God's kingdom and God's plan will be fulfilled in our lives. We need to go before the Lord in prayer, because the Bible points out that "we don't know what to pray for as we ought." We don't really know how to pray, and that's why the disciples begged, " Lord, teach us how to pray." They humbly recognized their need for God's help in all things, including prayer. Dr. Mark Hanby states, "You need to work out through prayer whatever is eating you. Otherwise, it will work

74

you out until nothing much is left of you. Work it out in prayer. Prayer is the key to revival. Let me repeat that: Prayer is the key to revival, to great revival. Great prayer brings great revival. Great singing will make you feel good and even make you think. Sometimes great singing also makes you weep and feel great emotion. Great preaching usually reaches great minds, but prayer reaches God. It's God whom you must reach."[3]

When we don't know what to pray for, the Holy Spirit will give us utterance. We need to let the Holy Ghost move in our hearts and souls. When you let the Holy Ghost get into your soul, moving upon your body, and letting Him take control of your tongue, He'll show you what to pray for with groanings that no man can utter. (See Rom. 8:26) We need to groan in the Spirit. There is something that God wants to birth in our communities, and we can't birth it by ourselves. In Chapter 12 of the book, "Family – How To Have A Healthy Christian Home," Marjorie Gordon states that, "We need to understand what prayer is so we can teach our children to pray. It is an invitation from God to talk to him in two-way conversation. God's part may be words from the Bible or a quiet voice in our thoughts. Our part should be as varied and enjoyable as talking with a good friend who is able to help us in every situation. Prayer is the evidence of our relationship between God and His children.[4] In order for these spiritual things to come forth, we've got to come together in a spirit of prayer, realizing that we're in this thing together -- all churches, age groups, races and communities united under God.

We need to begin to pray for revival.

For God I Live, and for God I Die

"And now for a little space grace hath been shewed from the Lord our God, to leave us a remnant to escape, and to give us a nail in His Holy place, that our God may lighten our eyes, and give us a little reviving in our bondage. For we were bondsmen; yet our God hath not forsaken us in our bondage, but hath

75

extended mercy unto us in the sight of the kings of Persia, to give us a reviving, to set up the house of our God, and to repair the desolation's thereof, and to give us a wall in Judah and in Jerusalem" (Ezra 9:8-9).

The revival that is coming is not just for young people. It is a revival for all of us. It is a revival for all the saints -- a revival that will change our communities, our homes, our families, our churches. It is a revival that moves beyond politics, moves beyond race, gender, age, denomination and the other things that divide people. It is a revival that will bring people of all backgrounds together. The revival declares, "For God I live, and for God I die."

It is a revival that speaks truth to the issues of life. It will enable us to stand up bodily and say, "Thus saith the Lord." This revival will bring back the voice of the prophets, an uncompromising voice that says, "I'm not ashamed of the Gospel of Jesus Christ, for I know it to be the power of God unto salvation." (See. Rom. 1:16)

The Gospel Is the Power of God

"Wilt thou not revive us again that thy people may rejoice in thee?" (Ps. 85:6)

If you want to know the power of prayer, the power of God, you will find it in the Gospel of Jesus Christ. When this reality from the Word of God comes alive in your life, you will know personal revival. The Bible says, "For I am not ashamed of the gospel of Christ: for it is the power of God unto salvation to every one that believeth" (Rom. 1:16).

So many folks are looking everywhere for the power. For example, they may go to an evangelist who will lay hands on their head. They may even go to some psychic for the help they seek. True power is found in the Gospel of Jesus Christ. If individuals are seeking someone to help them, they need to go to a person who is committed to the Gospel of Jesus Christ. They need to go to somebody who has integrity in the Lord. The Bible

76

warns, "Lay hands on no man suddenly." When we need the help of someone who has spiritual power, we need to go to somebody whose life is hid with Christ in God. Go to somebody who knows the Lord, and has a touch of God and then say, "Pray for me."

Oh, we've got to enter into prayer. We can no longer just talk about prayer, but this is something that we must do daily. We need to say, "Lord, teach me to pray. Lord, teach me the power of prayer, the fuel of revival."

God wants to give us His power. Sometimes my spiritual gas tank runs on empty, and sometimes I just keep pressing on and don't know how I'm going to make it. But then God gives me a word. Often that word is to pray. All the days of my life I'm going to get down on my knees and call on Him. I know there's power in the name of Jesus.

When I developed spinal meningitis, some doctors thought I would never walk again. Then some prayer warriors came in. They began to lay hands on me and to pray for me in the name of Jesus. Within a couple of hours I felt my legs begin to move. I said, "Doctor, I'm feeling better." The next morning I was discharged from the hospital. That following Sunday I was back in the pulpit preaching the gospel of Jesus Christ!

Oh, there's power available to us. If the Lord had decided not to heal me, I would still preach His Word. If I had to be in a wheelchair, I would still preach His Word. If I ended up on crutches, I would still preach His Word. If I had only one ounce of life in me, I would boldly declare that Jesus is my Lord.

When preachers begin to fail then the psychics rise up. God wants to raise up prophets for this day and hour. God wants to raise up apostles, pastors, teachers and evangelists who will show the world how to do this thing correctly.

Tarrying in Prayer

We're living in the last days. God wants to pour out His Spirit upon all the church. He's asking, "Would you tarry with me just a little while?" Tarrying in prayer involves so much more than a little sentence prayer. It truly is a life-style of prayer.

The Bible says, "But they that wait upon the Lord shall renew their strength; They shall mount up with wings as eagles; they shall run, and not be weary; and they shall walk, and not faint" (Isa. 40:3). If you want the power to be victorious, you have to learn how to wait on the Lord. Seek the Lord through prayer: "Lord, pull down my kingdoms; Lord, pull down the principalities in my life; Lord, pull down the strongholds in my life; pull down everything that's holding me back from being all that you want me to be." Surrender your life to the King of kings: "Here I am, Lord. I'm yours, Lord. Everything I am and everything I'm not is yours, Lord. Try me now and see if I can be completely yours."

If you have a personal relationship with the Lord, you may get into trouble, you may fall, you may mess up, but you can always call upon His Name, and He will answer.

Persistence in Prayer

Daniel prayed, but he didn't realize that the Lord had sent out angels to answer his prayer. The prince of Persia, a demon, was wrestling with the angel that was responding to his prayer. Prayer is more than a one-time thing, it is a matter of continued relationship with God.

Sometimes God sends down the blessing, and sometimes He is sending down the angels with the perfect answer, but along the way we may have to wrestle some demons. There are some demons that want to stop the blessing. The only way you can block the demons is if you're in continual relationship with God.

You need the power of God more than once. You need to avail yourself of God's power all the time -- through prayer. I don't want this to be only a one-time thing, but I've got to fill my gas tank daily. Every time it looks like it's getting anywhere near empty I need a new infilling.

Go to your spiritual gas station -- the place where you are accustomed to getting alone with God. For some folks this special place might be in the bathroom, as you're reading a devotional. For others, it might be in bed, at your bedside as you're reading your Bible. Some folks may go to their church early in the morning and get down on their knees. Wherever it is, you need to get alone with God, to constantly build upon your relationship with Him and to be filled with His power and glory.

You can't run on empty and think you're going to be victorious in your Christian life. We need the bread of life daily. We can't get all the Word of God in one day. That's why we need our daily dose. However, God teaches us some things daily. He can teach us about His power daily. He can teach us how to overcome daily. He can teach us how to succeed in the midst of failure daily. Let this be our constant prayer: "I'm pressing on the upward way, new heights I'm gaining each and every day. Lord, help me as I'm onward bound, Lord plant my feet on solid ground." In a *New York Times* article entitled "In Hope of Spiritual Revival, A Call To Fast," Bill Bright of Campus Crusade for Christ states that "Fasting and prayer are the atomic bomb, or the hydrogen bomb, of all the Christian disciplines,.... Prayer has great power, but fasting with prayer has infinitely more power."[10] *The New York Times*, Sunday, February 8, 1998, p1, In Hope of Spiritual Revival, "A Call to Fast."

Setting the Atmosphere for Revival

When my father, the late Rev. Dr. Arthur L. Mackey, Sr. was diagnosed with colon cancer which spread to the liver, we began a six a.m. prayer meeting lead Monday through Friday by Minister Patricia Brown. We still hold this meeting Monday through Friday and the results are tremendous. People are experiencing personal revival and coming closer to Christ. Prayer requests are coming in from all over. Reports of salvations, healings, and inner healings are pouring in. Six o'clock in the morning prayer might seem old fashioned to some, but having your most committed early morning prayer warriors interceding makes a major difference in laying the groundwork and setting the atmosphere for real revival.

Another type of prayer and praise meeting that sets the tone for real revival is the shut-in, an all night service. It works and gets the people of God focused and on one accord. For many years, our church had tried to build a new addition, and something would always go wrong. But when we began to hold shut-ins, God pulled down the spiritual strongholds that held us back. As Pastor and Pastor's wife, Brenda and I conduct shut-ins as often as possible, most importantly as the Holy Spirit leads. In fact, Psalms 134:1-3 speaks of a shut-in, an all night service that sets the atmosphere for real revival.

    1.)   Behold, bless ye the Lord, all ye servants of the Lord, which by night stand in the house of the Lord.

    2.)   Lift up your hands in the sanctuary, and bless the Lord.

    3.)   The Lord that made heaven and earth bless thee out of Zion.

Early morning Prayer, shut-ins, and rap sessions for the youth are only a few ways the Holy Spirit can use to set the atmosphere for real revival. The key is to continually seek God's face, and obey Him after you have prayed. It is not good enough to pray, we must also obey in order to experience real revival.

Ask and You Shall Receive

God says that if you're really serious about prayer, the fuel of revival, He will cause great things to happen. "Ask, and it shall be given you: seek, and ye shall find; knock, and it shall be opened unto you" (Matt. 7:7).

Someone might respond, "Well, Rev. Mackey, I prayed for my mother and she died." God answers, "And this is the confidence that we have in him, that, if we ask any thing according to his will, he heareth us: And if we know that he hears us, whatsoever we ask, we know that we have the petitions that we desired of him" (1 John 5:14-15).

Whatever we ask for in prayer, God points out that He wants us to ask according to His will. God has a will, He has a plan, and He has a destiny. Sometimes we may pray, "God, heal this person."

God may reply, *"I'm going to heal them,"* but He may give them a physical healing, or He might heal them by taking them to heaven -- truly the ultimate healing. If someone is in God's presence, he or she is truly healed.

God always answers prayer, but we don't always have the eyes to understand what He is doing. Truly effective revival prayer is when we pray God's word back to Him, or when we pray in the Holy Ghost.

His plan involves the power of prayer, which is the fuel of revival. Let's be a part of His great plan of the ages by getting to know Him through constant, persistent, personal prayer.

In many cases Alcoholism and sex outside of marriage has become the substitutes for prayer to wash the pain away, but Jesus wants to get you drunk in the Holy Spirit. He wants to fill you up with the new wine of the Holy Ghost, and show you what real revival and real living on the cutting edge of the Spirit of God is all about. Whatever you use to wash your pain away. Cry out "Revive Me Again". Cry out "Lord send a revival and let it begin in me." This is the road, the route with the best kicks, the road to real rejoicing.

Arthur L. Mackey, Jr.

Chapter 4

'REVIVE US AGAIN'-- THE ROAD TO REAL REJOICING

Real Revival Praise

To receive from God a word to share with you, the Holy Spirit led me again as He did in the introduction to Psalm 85. It is written to the sons of Korah, but today we want to address the sons and daughters of Christianity, the candidates of real revival.

The 85th division of Psalms reads, "Lord thou hast been favorable unto thy land, thou hast brought back the captivity of Jacob, thou hast forgiven the iniquity of thy people, thou has covered all their sin, *selah*. Thou hast taken away all thy wrath; thou hast turned thyself from the fierceness of thine anger. Turn us, oh God of our salvation, and cause thine anger toward us to cease. Wilt thou be angry with us forever? Wilt thou draw out thine anger to all generations? Wilt thou not revive us again; that thy people may rejoice in thee?

"Show us thy mercy, oh Lord, and grant us thy salvation. I will hear what God the Lord will speak; for He will speak peace unto His people, and to His saints; but let them not turn again to folly. Surely His salvation is nigh them that fear Him; that glory may dwell in our land. Mercy and truth are met together; righteousness and peace have kissed each other.

"Truth shall spring out of the earth; and righteousness look down from heaven. Yea, the Lord shall give that which is good; and our land yield her increase. Righteousness shall go before him; and shall set us in the way of His steps." May the Lord add a blessing to the reading of His Word, and sanctify it accordingly within our hearts.

Arthur L. Mackey, Jr.

Okay, let us look again at that sixth verse: "Wilt thou not revive us again; that thy people may rejoice in thee?" God wants to give you real revival praise.

Praying for Revival

I like to lift up the following subject: "Revive Us Again." Revive us again, concerning the need for revival prayer, because that is a burden that is upon my heart, to call the people of God together to pray. To pray for real revival, to pray for that quest, that journey, for spiritual renewal to occur in our lives. We need it in order to impact our community, and make a difference in our world, in our community, and in our families. We need it in order to be able to impact our communities in a positive manner and to make a difference in the lives of our people who are suffering. Our people are hurting right now, and some of the problems are out of our league. Some of the problems are out of our control. We need some divine intervention. Oh yes, we can go to the jails, and we can go to the hospitals, and there is so much that we can do. But some of the problems reach a point where there is nothing that we can do. Only God can step in and intervene.

That's why we need to ask Him to step in and intervene in the affairs of men, the affairs of women, and boys and girls, to turn the situation around. We don't have the power to turn the situation around, but if God touches the life of a man, if God touches the life of a woman, if God touches the life of a little girl, or a little boy, He can turn their lives around. Psalms 85:3-4 states that "Thou hast taken away all thy wrath: thou hast turned thyself from the fierceness of thine anger. Turn us, O God of our salvation, and cause thine anger toward us to cease." God's got the power to save our community, God's got the power to save our boys, and God's got the power to save our girls.

84

Natural Examples of Revival

Revive Us Again. I am talking about Holy Ghost revival. There are many different forms of revival, earthly examples of revival in every day life. For example, let's say that you go and see a great play and you give it an outstanding review. Then others experience that wonderful play. And people begin to talk about it. People begin to write about it. Critics on television, and on the radio, and in the newspaper begin to discuss it. Then there is a demand for that play to come back again. It experiences a natural revival. Revival is not limited to top notch Broadway plays, but God wants His church to experience real supernatural revival in the deepest recesses of our soul that calls the church to turn from its wicked ways.

Renowned Christian author Fushia Pickett addresses the question: "Are We Headed Toward Revival? Prayer is what precipitates a nation-changing revival. Thank God He is calling the church to prayer! Surely He would not call His people to pray for the nation if our ills were incurable. All across this nation more and more believers are repenting of their prayerlessness and lifting their voices to God - that's why I believe we are in the beginning stages of Revival". [1]

Many forms of revival that are present, are evident in our society. Just a few years ago, Diana, Princess of Wales, had everything to live for. She was enjoying a budding romance, even though her marriage had ended. Suddenly one day she was riding in an automobile with Doty Alfiad and the paparazzi began to chase them. I'm not sure if the driver was drunk or not. But somehow they crashed into a wall.

There was a great outpouring of sympathy. Everybody was talking about Princess Di--the way that she prayed, the way she walked, talked and comforted AIDS patients. She was a caring person. My wife, Brenda, and I were in London conducting a revival. Members at the church we were ministering at told us that they "just love Princess Di, because she's so down to earth. If you see her on the street she will speak to you. But some of

85

the other royals have their noses up in the air, and they are too high and mighty to relate to the common people."

So when she was killed in that accident, there was an outcry of sympathy. In essence, there was a call for an earthly revival. When they looked at Prince William and Prince Harry they wanted a little bit of Princess Diana to come back again. They said of Prince William and Prince Harry, "Don't be too uppity," but revival will have to come through them. What are you trying to say? We want you to keep that fire burning. Oh, don't let the king or the queen, or anybody else let that fire that Diana lit go out. We want you to keep it burning, we want that revival to continue."

After the death of Princess Diana we heard about the death of Mother Teresa, who really loved people. She understood the meaning of compassion--one who would go out into the streets and deal with the lepers, and love them, and care for them. It wasn't just mere words. She put action behind her words. She knew that faith without works is dead. She knew how to care. She knew how to share. She knew how to reach out to the less fortunate and to those who were suffering.

But as I was watching the funeral on television and they talked about the order that she was in charge of, they also said that there was a new nun who would take this position. As that new nun took that position, they hoped for a real revival. Because Mother Teresa would go out and get money for the mission, they wanted that work to go on. They wanted a revival in the midst of the years.

My third child, baby Faith, wakes up at three o' clock in the morning and wants to be changed and fed. Then her little brother Jordan hears her cry, and begins to cry for a bottle. It is all a natural revival of the times years ago that I spent with my first daughter, Yolanda, when she was a new born. I changed her diapers and fed her baby milk formula. Yolanda, who is in 1st grade, now sleeps through the night. She occasionally gets up after her sister and brother. These days my time with Yolanda is spent tickling her and playing hide and go seek, singing her favorite songs that she learned on the school bus, doing homework with her, reading books, watching the Rugrats and the Brady Bunch--her favorite shows (as well as a bunch of other cartoons), and learning John 3:16 and other Bible verses. We are experiencing the revival that God has for us as father and daughter as we ride to Wendy's. I get the "Garden Pita" and she gets the kid's meal and just wants to play with the toy. I have to remind her to eat the food.

The people of God are called to realize that God wants to bring a real revival into our lives--a revival that impacts our lives spiritually, relationally, and financially.

God wants to bring a genuine spiritual renewal into our homes. He wants to bring a move that will transform our homes, a move that will transform our community, a move that will transform our schools. God wants to breathe on us with real revival and Holy Ghost fire.

Deliverance Out of Captivity

So as we study at Psalms 85, we see that the sons of Korah received a word from the Lord, a word that we can share with the sons and the daughters of Atlanta, New York, L.A., Detroit and all other cities. We must share with the sons and the daughters of Africa, England, China and other countries as well. We thank God that there is a word from the Lord to revive us in the midst of our tears. God wants to revive us in the midst of our fears, to revive us in the midst of our heartache and pain. Lord, revive us again. The first verse of Psalm 85 says, "Lord, thou hast been favorable unto thy land and hath brought back the captivity of Jacob." This is talking about the children of Israel being held captive in Babylon, and the Lord delivering them out of that captivity.

There is a captivity in your life that God wants to deliver you out of. You know, that thing that is holding you back from all that God wants you to be! Deliverance is one aspect of the sovereign move of God. I want to deal with that aspect of deep, cleansing deliverance, that aspect of God bringing you out of the pit of deep despair and depression.

True deliverence from depression is a result of personal revival prayer. Passionate prayer will revive your deprived spirit and rekindle the deep desire to be free from bondage. That burning desire for deliverence and the freedom in Christ that it brings is the revival of the wounded spirit and soul.

Oh, there may have been somebody who cursed somebody out. They won't admit it but they may have thought it. You may have done it, too. But the Lord wants to bring you out. There may have been somebody who had a problem, and you picked up a liquor bottle to wash away your problems. But God is saying, "I have some inner counseling for you. I have some healing for you that can bring you through the problem better than any liquor bottle. I want to revive your wounded spirit and bring you out."

The legendary Rev. Dr. Gardener C. Taylor closed out a sermon that best reflects our situation, *A promise for life's long pull.* "Sometimes I feel discouraged and think my works in vain'.....but then, just when my strength seems spent and gone; then when I come almost to the borders of despair, when I feel frustrated and confused and out of it—Then...the Holy Spirit comes and 'Revives my soul again.'" [2]

There may be some woman, or some man who wants to get you into a relationship that you know you shouldn't be in. But God says, "I want to bring you out of your Babylon." No matter what your personal Babylon is, I want to deliver you from captivity, from thoughts that you know aren't right. But God is going to deal with it. Yes, God will bring you out, if you let Him....

"Trust in the Lord, and lean not unto thine own understanding, and He will direct thy path." Say, "Direct my path, Lord, in my home. Direct my path, Lord, at my job. Direct my path, Lord, in my community. Direct my path, Lord, in the church. Direct my path, Lord, as I talk to my wife. Direct my path, as I talk to my children. Direct my path, Lord. Touch me. Do it one more time. Revive me in the Name of Jesus."

Revive us again.

The Source of Our Strength

What is the purpose for God's reviving us? That we may truly learn how to rejoice in Him. The book of Nehemiah says that "The joy of the Lord is my strength." When we learn to praise and worship God we are blessed by praise and worship. It says, "The joy of the Lord is our strength." When we truly praise and worship God, that gives the heart of God joy. And when the heart of God receives joy, He gives us strength.

He says, "They're really praising Me. I'm going to give them strength to make it through their personal problems." Someone died and God says, "Well, they're praising Me through their problem. I'm going to give them strength. I'm going to give them power to make it." This one thought that they would backslide and give up, but they're praising Me. Oh, come on! I'm going to throw a little strength down there so they can make it through their journey."

"The joy of the Lord is our strength." That's one of the purposes of revival, that we may learn to rejoice in Him through the struggle and through the pain. Learn to rejoice in Him through the tribulation, because weeping may endure for a night, but joy comes in the morning.

Mercy and Salvation

Let us look back into the Word of the Lord, the 7th verse says, "Show us thy mercy, oh Lord, and grant us thy salvation." The salvation of God, is not just in terms of receiving Him as the Lord our Savior. That is an aspect of salvation, but salvation includes deliverance throughout our entire life. Every struggle, everything that we go through, God gives us deliverance power to bring us through situations until we see Him face to face in glory.

Arthur L. Mackey, Jr.

Hear What God Speaks

The eighth verse says, "I will hear what God the Lord will speak." Many times we don't hear what God is saying. We want to hear what we've got to say about the problem. But it says, "I will hear God, the Lord." Not just God the Savior, because He can be the Savior of our lives while we are living in sin. Say, "Lord, I've still got some problems, I've still got some hang-ups, I've still got some hurts. But now you're my Lord of revival. You're in charge and you're the one who does the driving. If I want to go this way and you say 'No, go that way,' that's the way I'm going. You're in the driver's seat right now."

Hallelujah. Revive Us Again.

Peace Unto His People

"He will speak peace unto His people." In a genuine revival God doesn't give only deliverance. He speaks peace, words of inner healing, eternal hope and comfort. You can be brought out of a situation, but if you don't receive God's peace that passes all understanding, you may go back into the same thing again. "He will speak peace unto His people."

Let me submit this to you: A real, genuine revival is not just a week's worth of services with some preacher or choirs. It's the continuous work of the Holy Spirit that God does in the lives of the people of God. So when the sinner sees the people of God, he too may fear. The spirit of God will come upon him and repent of his sins. God will speak peace to His people.

Someone may have been raped. Someone may have been sexually abused, or verbally abused. God wants to speak peace - inner healing and essential wholeness to His people. Oh, you may have been going through a situation that you never thought you could make it through, but "God, wants to speak peace to His people." [3]

Or, you thought that you wouldn't have survived. You thought you would give up. But God wants to speak peace and inner healing to His people. God speaks to that hurting place, where the pain is too much to bear and you think that you could never go on. In genuine revival, God not only gives deliverance; He wants to give you peace. Bishop Eddie Long states, "We can't let despair overwhelm us. After all, you can't resurrect something unless it's dead. If we didn't have problems, we wouldn't need revival. I am not excited about the problems we still face, but I am excited that God is acting to overcome them!"[4]

No Turning Back

Let's go on in the Word of the Lord to His saints: "Let them not turn again to folly." God doesn't want us to take for granted the deliverance, the peace and the inner healing that He brings into our life and just take it lightly.

We're living in the last days. There are numbers in the Bible that mean many significant things: 40 days and 40 nights… and the 120 believers in the upper room who received the initial outpouring of the baptism of the Holy Spirit on the day of Pentecost. But the number three is very significant in the Bible. The year 2000 marked the approaching of the third day, the third millennium, since the life, death, and resurrection of Jesus Christ. I'm not saying that Jesus is going to come back then, but I'm saying that we're closer to it than we were a thousand years ago. And we're living in a generation when it could happen.

The Bible has prophecies that say that everyone will know about it instantly around the world. We have cable news networks, CNN, Fox News, and many others where those prophecies can be instantly revealed; we're living in the fig tree generation. We have got to believe God for real, genuine revival. I'm not just talking about some big spiritual thing that we can't relate to, but real down-to- earth revival in our home. If you want God's deliverance, if you want God's peace, learn to pray with your families first.

If you want God's deliverance, if you want God's peace, His inner healing, learn to pray when you go into the bathroom. Stop worrying about the problems. If we want God's deliverance, if we want God's peace learn to pray when we're riding in the car. If we want inner healing, God's deliverance, let real revival prayer be a continual thing. "Revive us Again."

Turn to Habakkuk the third chapter and the second verse. It says, "Lord, I have heard thy speech and was afraid; oh Lord revive thy work in the midst of the years. In the midst of wrath, remember mercy."

Mercy and Truth, Righteousness and Peace Double Date

You see, when God brings genuine revival we will know it because it will spread like wild fire. When we get a real move of God, when God's spirit begins to move, mercy and truth come together, righteousness and peace kiss. During revival mercy, which is concerned with forgiveness, comes together with truth. Mercy tells the truth, focusing on the eternal truth that we are forgiven. What is always right and correct even when we were wrong gets together with peace that tries to keep everything calm. They begin to kiss. They begin to hug. They begin to get romantic, because they're not opposing forces. They are forces that are ordained by God to make sure that His real, genuine revival will come forth. And not only will righteousness and peace get together, ah, but mercy and truth already have hooked them up.

The same thing happens in our relationship with God. When we're in right standing with Him, that represents true righteousness. And when righteousness joins up with peace and mercy with truth, the tranquillity of inner healing becomes evident. But when you join it all together, do you know what it equals? It equals a work of God being done at your home. It equals a work of God being done in your life. It equals a work of God being done in your spirit.

No Cowardly Soldiers

Say, "Lord, I want you to do a work in my life. Lord, I know that you don't want any coward soldiers. And Lord, I won't be a coward soldier." Say, "I am not ashamed of the gospel of Jesus Christ, for it is the power, it is the power, it is the power, it is the power that I need for revival. It is the power that I need for restoration. It is the power that I need for inspiration. It is the power that I need for motivation." Lift up your hands and say, "Lord, revive me. Lord, recharge me. Lord, renew me. Lord, revitalize me. Lord, revamp me. Lord, rekindle the fire. Let the fire burn in my home. Let the fire burn on my job. Lord, sometimes I hear folk blessing your Name, and I don't know what to say. Teach me to praise your Name on the job, even if I do it quietly. Teach me to have a Christian witness, even if it's a silent Christian witness. Let them see something in me. Let them see through my actions that Jesus is living here. Lord, do a work. Lord, send a move. Help me to witness to my friends. Help me to witness to my enemies. Help me to go on even when I feel like giving up. Help me to go on when I feel like throwing in the towel. Bring me through the struggle in the Name of Jesus."

When I was 13 years old, the Lord laid it on my heart to start a Bible study in Roosevelt High School, and also at my home. Although I taught Bible study in the high school, God may have something different for you to do. God has plenty of ideas and inspiration but you have to seek Him for direction. We don't need just good ideas. We need God-ordained ideas, ideas ordained and predestined by God to make a real difference.

There are things that God is speaking to the hearts of people and God wants to do a revival in your lives. Remember that time when you were truly on fire for God. God doesn't want us to be lukewarm. It's not just in the dance. It's not just in the shout. It's in the doing. All we need is just a little reviving.

93

Arthur L. Mackey, Jr.

PART TWO:

THE ULTIMATE

REVIVALIST-JESUS CHRIST

Chapter 5

LORD OF REVIVAL - HE IS SOVEREIGN

In this chapter I would like to discuss the subject, "The Lord of Revival." Let us examine closely the subject. In order for real revival to occur, we must be concerned about doing the work of the Lord for the cause of revival. But more importantly, we must know in an intimate way the Lord of revival personally. God is concerned about lost souls who were once submitted to His will, wisdom, and way.

Recently my six year old Yolanda woke up early on Sunday morning and said, "Daddy, my first tooth fell out." This was a very special moment. As I went to embrace her as she showed me the tooth and put it in my hand, suddenly I saw my two year old son Jordan breaking up his mother's necklace. I instantly turned around to stop Jordan, and dropped the tooth. Yolanda and I searched for two hours straight before church for the tooth, but to no avail. Finally I looked in the jewelry box from which Jordan had taken the necklace. Lo and behold, there was the lost tooth hidden underneath the pieces of broken necklace.

Jesus Christ, Lord of Revival, cares even more for one lost soul that is reclaimed and revived from a backslidden lifestyle and returns to the fold to enjoy fellowship with the saints.

In the book of Habakkuk, God gives us some insights concerning the true meaning of revival. In Habakkuk the third chapter, verses one and two state, "A prayer of Habakkuk the prophet, upon Shigionoth. Oh Lord, I have heard thy speech, and was afraid; oh Lord revive thy work in the midst of the years, in the midst of the years make known; in wrath remember mercy."

Now in the book of Habakkuk we must realize that Habakkuk had a burden for the people of Judah who were being oppressed by the Chaldeans (Babylonians) because of their disobedience to God. He was troubled by the calamity, by the pain, by the pressure and violence of his day. Habakkuk 1:1,2 says, "The burden which Habakkuk the prophet did see. Oh Lord, how long shall I cry and thou wilt not hear, even cry out unto thee of violence, and thou wilt not save?"

Now let's take a look at that very closely. "The burden which Habakkuk the prophet did see." There was a heavy weight, a burden, a huge rock, a boulder that Habakkuk could see in the spiritual realm. This weight, this burden, this heavy load represented the violence, the hatred, the spirit of evil that had arisen in Judah. And Habakkuk was concerned about his community, the same way that we would be concerned about our community. When babies are having babies, when there are drive-by shootings, when gangs begin to proliferate and begin to spread greatly throughout the community. "Help!" But nobody comes to save.

In his classic book, "The Purpose Driven Church–Growth Without Compromising Your Message And Mission," Dr. Rick Warren, the Senior Pastor of Saddleback Valley Community Church in Orange County, California, states that, "Even many politicians are coming to the conclusion that spiritual revival is our only solution."[1]

Habakkuk had a burden, a cry of compassion and concern to see a change come about. He wanted something to be done about the violence. He wanted something to be done about this pain and the danger that the people of Judah found themselves in. The Word says that he cried out to God and asked the question, "How long?" He could not understand why God would allow the Chaldeans (Babylonians) to punish Judah. Before it was all over, God also punished the Babylonians. What God allows is not the same as what God wants. So you cannot use these scriptures to justify slavery or oppression.

97

Arthur L. Mackey, Jr.

How Long Lord?

In today's society, we ask the question, "How long? How long, Lord, will injustice occur? How long will the crime continue to plaque our society? How long will we reap abuse, including verbal, sexual and mental? How long, Lord?

And he cried out and said, "God, do you hear what I'm saying?" And he cried out to God concerning the violence.

Two V's—"Violence" and "Vision"

So Habakkuk raises up one word with a V: "violence". But God responds to Habakkuk with another word that begins with a V. God gives to Habakkuk the same word that He gives to us today, and that is "vision". God responds to the violence and turmoil in present-day society by giving men and women of God a vision of victory to turn the situation around. If we take care of the business that God has put in our hands, He will take care of the rest because God alone is sovereign.

Now, in the second chapter of Habakkuk's book, verses one through four, it says: "I will stand upon my watch, and set me upon the tower. I will watch to see what he will say unto me, and I shall answer when I am reproved. And the Lord answered me and said, Write the vision, and make it plain upon the tables, that he may run that readeth it. For the vision is yet for an appointed time, but at the end it shall speak and not lie; though it tarry, wait for it; because it will surely come, it will not tarry. Behold, his soul which is lifted up is not upright in him, but the just shall live by faith."

Now let's back up for a minute. In the second chapter, first verse, Habakkuk says, "I will stand upon my watch and will set me upon the tower. I will watch to see what he will say unto me, and what I shall answer when I am reproved."

In the first chapter the prophet shares his burden. He had great doubt concerning the hand of God in the midst of the violence that was going on. In essence he was saying, "Where are you, God? You're silent, You're not doing anything. Are you there? Are you concerned? Do you have any compassion? Do you care at all?" And so he realizes that God is going to respond and answer him and deal with his heartache and pain concerning the injustices of the society he lived in. He was somewhat afraid that he would be rebuked by God. He was wondering what type of answer God would give him. Would He strike him down for asking such questions? Many times we are afraid to ask God questions concerning painful situations that have occurred in our lives.

The Answer to Prayer

Prayer is dialogue with God. God wants us to talk to Him. He wants us to be honest and speak to Him as our heavenly Father, and to move into a more personal and intimate communication with Him. Call Him "Abba Father," "our Father," "our Father which art in heaven." He wants us to realize the magnitude of that relationship, that our heavenly Father is concerned about us, and that He will move in our lives.

So God answers Habakkuk, in the second chapter, second verse: "And the Lord answered me." When we talk to God, God will answer. The answer may not always be what we want. Sometimes the answer to a prayer is yes, and sometimes the answer to a prayer is no. Sometimes the answer to a prayer is wait. The Bible says, "They that wait upon the Lord shall renew their strength; they will mount up with wings like eagles, they will run and not get weary, they will walk and not faint."

In the church, all too often we emphasize that the answer to a prayer is the answer that you want to get. But that's not always true. Many times God will answer a prayer, and we will think that the prayer has not been answered because the way we want it to be answered has not come to pass. In our reality, if we look closely, God has sent an answer. His answer is always consistent with His Word.

We might want to go to one location, and God decides to send us to another location, but God is faithful. He knows what is best. God is a healer, and a deliverer. He will always stay true to His Word.

So the Lord answers Habakkuk and tells him, in essence: "I realize what you're saying about the violence, and yes, this is true. But you've given me that big V word 'violence,' which is a reality. I can tell that the people's lives are being devastated by the violence. But I want to give you a word: 'vision.'"

The Vision of Victory

God is calling on men and women all across this world to be people of vision, to catch His vision of victory and never give up. He wants us to take the vision into the prisons, the streets, the ghettos and foreign lands. Equally important, God's vision of victory will change our lives, it will allow the fire of God to take root and burn in our hearts, and burn in our souls. We will no longer come up with our own ideas and our own concepts. We will develop a God consciousness where we are led by the Spirit of God to have an impact on society. The center of society will see a change in our lives. As a result, real revival will begin to break out in the churches, because saints will look at other saints who have been convicted by the Holy Spirit to stop living in sin, living beneath their privileges as believers in Jesus Christ.

So the Word goes on and says, "The Lord answered me and said, Write the vision." We must realize that the vision that God gives to us must be written down. When we realize the vision, the plan, the idea or the concept that God gives to us, and we write His vision down, we're making a contract between God and ourselves. What we are actually saying is, "Lord of revival, this is what you said, and I know that you're able to perform it. I know that you're able to bring it to pass."

And after we write the vision it instructs, "Make it plain." God doesn't want us to add anything to His Word, or take anything away from His Word. If God gives you a vision, write down what God told you. Let it be plain. Let it be clear and concise, because God is not going to speak in mumble-jumble. God is going to give you a clear message, and clear direction.

Pray, "Lord, let my steps be ordered by you," and He will direct your footsteps. As God gives you that clear vision of victory, you have to write it down to make sure that you put it down just the way God said it. If you put it down just the way God said it, the message is going to be clear. There will be no confusion.

And it says, the purpose of this is "so that the person who reads about what God has said, can run with it." People need a vision of victory. People need a plan that they can run with. See, if we don't get a vision of victory, eventually we're going to latch on to someone else's vision, plan, dream, or concept. If we don't receive a vision of victory from God for our families, then our children will begin to receive a vision from the gangs, because they haven't received a vision from God that has been brought forth from the mouth of the father and the mother.

If our church leaders don't receive a vision of victory from God, then the members of the churches are going to go elsewhere to receive the vision. They might call the psychic networks, or they might go to soothsayers, or just gossip on the phone, bickering, back biting, trying to find a vision in all the wrong places. So it's important to have a vision of victory. God is dealing with Habakkuk about vision. There is something more profound that He wants to bring him into, and that is real, genuine, authentic revival. God wants to rekindle flames of revival in the hearts of believers all across this world. Think about the great Azusa Street revival in the early 1900s and the work that God did through William Seymour, a praying man. It's astonishing how they got together in that old building. And they began to worship God and speak in other tongues. They gave God all glory, honor and praise. That one revival was the foundation for the modern Pentecostal movement in American society. Not only was Seymour a praying man, a leader of the original Azusa street revival in the early 1900s' he also expressed his view on authentic revival.

"We find where men and women have received this baptism with the spirit there is a revival going on, just as on the day of Pentecost. That is what the baptism of the spirit means-continual revival."[2]

Let Your Little Light Shine

God can light a flame in your heart and that little light is yours. Remember the song, "This little light of mine, I'm going to let it shine." That little light in your heart, can help someone else to catch on fire. It can become wildfire that can bring forth real revival--first in your home, then in your Bible study, your local church, your local community, then maybe in your state, throughout the nation and throughout the world.

No revival prayer is in vain, no Bible study is in vain, no Godly effort to witness to lost souls is in vain if we are hooked up and connected with the Lord of revival.

Now God deals with Habakkuk some more about the vision of victory and preparation for what He's going to say to him concerning His work, the move of His Spirit, Habakkuk's concerns, and finally his response to what God is going to say. At first he thought that he might respond in anger, or he just was afraid in terms of what God would say.

But now the Lord has Habakkuk's attention and explains to him that the vision is for an appointed time. The vision will not happen overnight. God has a clock and a time table. In His perfect time, this plan, sent straight from the mind of God, shall come to pass. But God's ways are not our ways, and God's thoughts are not our thoughts. As high as the heaven is from the earth, so high are God's ways from our ways.

A Person of Vision

So God has His own clearly made decision when this is going to come to pass. We cannot make it happen in our own time. That is negative and ungodly. The only thing that God wants us to truly make happen is to wait on Him, minister unto

102

Him and for Him everywhere we go. Now in many cases people claim to be waiting on God, but the truth really is that God is waiting on them, because they that wait on the Lord of revival shall renew their strength. They shall mount up with wings like eagles. They shall run and not get weary, they shall walk and not faint.

You know what God wants us to make happen? It is to rest in Him. If you want God's best, enter into His rest. Nike says, "Just do it! If you really want to be motivational, and just do it, just learn to wait on God, worship and praise through word and action day by day." If you really want to be a person who is a mover and a shaker, and a great motivator, I'll tell you what to do to make it happen. Trust in the Lord; lean not to your own understanding, and He will direct your path.

If you really want to be a person of vision who makes things happen, I'll tell you what to do. Humble yourself. The Bible didn't say wait for God to humble you. But, humble yourself, make it happen, humble yourself. It only takes one person to get on fire for Jesus and light a torch of truth that will start a wild fire of revival.

The Holy Spirit has been working on your heart for a long time, He's been convicting you a mighty long time. Just do this: "Humble yourself under the mighty hand of God, then He will exalt you in due time." It only takes one positive person who is truly yielded to God, who is willing to make things happen and allow God to minister through them to reach others for Christ.

Many times we try to make the wrong things happen. The things that God tells us to make happen are to wait on Him, praise Him, worship Him, witness, preach, teach, share His love every single day. The things that God tells us to make happen are to trust in Him, yield to Him, and spread His word, because in Him we live and move and have our being. If you want the best, enter the rest. Get on fire for God with His vision to reach the lost. Humble yourself, pay your bills, tithe, give offerings, witness, walk in love, and occupy by the leading of the Holy Spirit until He comes.

Some things we cannot make happen. We can only make happen what God has empowered us to do, one day at a time. For example, we can pray in faith, but only God can heal. We can pray and witness to the lost, but only Jesus can change their lives. You see, when you put it into proper perspective there are things that the Lord of revival wants you to witness and share. Things that only he can do. We can try in our flesh, but we always fail and yearn for the real touch of God. Promotion doesn't come from the east, nor the west, but promotion comes from the Lord of revival.

This Vision Has A Voice

As we look at this, God says to him that "The vision is for an appointed time." You cannot do it yourself. God has to do it. He says, "But at the end, this vision is going to speak." This vision has a voice of its own. But in order to hear the voice of this vision of victory you must know God as Lord of the Bible. Don't get caught up in merely dealing with the work of the Lord. You can experience burn out in ministry, burn out in the things of God. You can end up drowning in shallow waters, but you must realize that the vision shall speak and not tarry. Develop patience and there will come a point when God will step in, and that vision of victory shall come to pass. It's going to speak louder than words. In its fulfillment everyone will see that this is a work that God has established. This was done by the Lord of revival. He is Sovereign. God is in control.

So the verse continues, "and it will not lie." The vision of victory that God sends concerning His real revival is not a lie. God is not a man, a foolish, stupid man that He would lie. No, no, no. God doesn't come down to that level. He is the Lord of revival. He is the eternal revivalist.

Wait for the Vision

He tells us to wait for the vision of victory, because it will surely come.

Now early in the verse it said, "Though it tarry...." There is a time in which there will be a period of waiting, and we've got to wait. But then He says, "It will surely come." If God gives you a vision of victory, if it's actually sent from the Lord of revival, if it's sent from the corridors of glory, it will come to pass.

Now I want to deal with this 4th verse. It says, "Behold his soul which is lifted up is not upright in him." Meaning that when this vision of victory comes to pass, God begins to do a great work of real revival in your life. Your soul is being lifted up by God. You're being elevated and brought to a new place and relationship in God. You're not upright in yourself and you did not make this happen. The only thing that you made happen was humbling yourself, submitting yourself and taking action, moving where God says to go. But the exalting came from God.

God Alone Is Sovereign

If God says to humble yourself, write that vision. If God says to seek Him, write that vision, make it plain, that the person that reads it can run with it. Then God is the one who brings forth the motion. God is the one who does the exalting.

Now listen to this: "Behold, the soul which is lifted up is not upright in Him." It's not upright in Him, but it's upright only through God. Without God, without the blood of Jesus, we're nothing but filthy rags. But with the blood of Jesus, we receive a covering and we receive a cleansing where we become the righteousness of God in Christ Jesus.

So there is no goodness of our own. In the flesh there is no good thing. The only good thing about us is the cleansing and the covering that we receive from the blood of Jesus. We have to be conscious of this, and we have to remember this so we do not become spiritually arrogant and think that we are the ones who are doing it. No, it's only by the grace of God. No matter what work He's called you to do, it's only by the grace of God that we are alive right now.

105

'The Just Shall Live By Faith'

The Bible says, "But the just shall live by faith." If you really want to know the Lord of revival, if you really want Him to do a work in your life, you must realize that the just person, the Christian person, the believer must live by faith. This is a daily faith walk in hard times, as well as in good times. With this faith we must have the vision that God has given to us.

We must seek Him, we must humble ourselves before Him, run with the vision and share His love. This is something we've got to do daily. We've got to deal with our ego daily. We've got to deal with our attitudes daily. When we know that we want to tell a person off, we've got to seek God's face to ask His direction in terms of how to deal with this. We know we want to be firm in different situations. We want to come across in the right manner, but we need to be seasoned with the salt of the Holy Spirit so the words that we speak, can bring healing, and correction. They can bring discipline and they can bring words of wholeness. More importantly, they can also help people's lives. But they have to be words that are seasoned by the Holy Spirit, seasoned by the Lord of revival.

Eavesdropping on God and the Prophet

What's the whole reason for this? Why does God deal with a vision in talking to Habakkuk? God is so gracious He allows us to eavesdrop on the conversation via the Bible. We are able to eavesdrop on a conversation between God and Habakkuk--a conversation that He did not have to make us privy to, but He has recorded it so we can be blessed.

Why did God give an answer concerning the violence of Habakkuk's day in Judah? Why did God deal with the vision? And why goes he go on and deal with the subject of faith, preparing us for revival? Why did the Lord of revival answer in this form and in this fashion?

106

Covering the Earth with His Glory

Well the reason is given in the 14th verse: "For the earth shall be filled with the knowledge of the glory of the Lord [the Lord of revival] as the waters cover the sea." That is what God desires, that the earth be filled with the knowledge of the glory of God.

And believers are doing this with books, tapes, and sermons, but it goes even further than that--it has to be done through changed lives. The books... the tapes... the sermons... the videos... the CDs--all are tools that God can use to motivate, to bring people into the kingdom and to help us experience revival in our lives. But the bottom line is changed lives, saved souls, spirits that are rekindled with the fire of the Holy Ghost. It spreads like wildfire. Every single chance they get, saying that they're not ashamed of the gospel of Jesus Christ, for it is the power of God. It's the good news that Jesus is risen from the dead, that He lives, that He died, and that He has risen from the dead. He is present. He is alive right now to do a marvelous work in anyone's life who needs Him. That is power. That is the power of God unto salvation for the guy who is out on the street corner with drugs. It's salvation for the man or the woman, the boy or the girl who has trouble putting down the liquor bottle. It's salvation for the one who's addicted to sex. It's salvation for the one who's addicted to lying. It's salvation for the one who's addicted to cheating. God's Word of the gospel represents power. It is power and it will bring forth deliverance to anyone who believes it. God wants to spread the knowledge of this fact.

God wants that knowledge to glorify Him through changed lives, saved souls, and rekindled spirits. He wants us to cover the earth like the waters cover the sea. That is the vision that God wants to drop into the hearts and minds of billions of people throughout the world.

So when the last person hears the gospel and receives that message, and the gospel has been preached throughout all the nations, then Jesus can return. He wants this message of real revival that births effective evangelism to spread. Be obedient. Just do it where you are. Start with witnessing one on one.

God is calling His people to realize that He's not like a dumb stone, that He is not like an idol, He is not some religious relic that people pray to. A religious relic that hates real revival, never answers, nor does a statue of stone ever answer. He is not Buddha. He is not Mohammed. He is the Lord of revival and He alone is sovereign.

The Lord of Revival Is In His Holy Temple

Habakkuk 2:20 says, "The Lord is in His holy temple."

Today in the new covenant, our body is the temple of God. The Lord of revival is in His Holy temple. You shut up and listen to God.

"Now the other idols, religious relics, if they were people living during their lifetime, are dead. But the Lord of revival is in His holy temple. Jesus is alive and well and He calls all the earth to keep silence before Him. The church can lift up His Name, praise Him, dance and shout. But He calls the earth to keep silence before Him, to give Him His due respect, "For the earth is the Lord's and the fullness thereof, the world, and they that dwell therein."

Singing a Prayer That Births Revival

The 3rd chapter of Habakkuk says that "A prayer of Habakkuk the prophet upon Shigionoth" represents a song. In other words, the prayer that Habakkuk prayed in this 3rd chapter he sang as a prayer unto the Lord. When was the last time you sang a prayer unto the Lord? Does it represent revival occurring in your life?

In the 1st chapter of Habakkuk, the prophet had great doubt. He was concerned about the violence; his prayer to God was a prayer of doubt. And we should not be afraid to talk to God even in times of doubt. We might as well go on and talk to Him. We know that Habakkuk had his doubts but he still talked to God.

And now, in the 3rd chapter, we can see that after God has responded, Habakkuk received the Word of the Lord and his faith was increased. We can see a difference in the way that Habakkuk responds to God. If we talk to God even in the midst of our doubts, our pains, our heartaches, if we honestly cry out unto the Lord, He will answer. He may not always answer the way that we want Him to answer, but He'll give us the best answer. He'll give us the answer that we truly need.

So the 2nd verse says, "Oh Lord" [I love this], "I have heard thy speech." In other words, he's saying, "I've heard everything that you said. Your response to my questions about the violence of the day, the turmoil of the day, the heartache and pain of the day, and I've heard your speech concerning vision." And he says, "I was afraid."

But then Habakkuk responds by saying, "Revive your work." So he says, "Revive thy work." Habakkuk realizes that this is the work of God. This isn't his work. This isn't something that he can make happen. The only good thing God wants him to make happen is prayer. He wants him to commit himself to prayer because He has empowered him through the Holy Spirit to pray. But he says, "Revive thy work." He realizes that it's only God who can bring real revival. It is "not by might or by power, but by my spirit" says the Lord of revival. Habakkuk realizes that I cannot bring this genuine revival on myself. We cannot make real revival happen, but we can humble ourselves, pray, seek His face and turn from our wicked ways. The Lord of revival will in turn heal the land and send real revival. There are things that I can do that God has told me to do--to humble myself, to seek His face. "If My people which are called by My Name shall humble themselves and pray, and seek My face, and turn from their wicked ways, then will I hear from heaven and forgive their sins, and heal their land."

I can do that but only God can heal the land. I can humble myself. I can pray. I can seek His face. I can do those things but only God can heal the land. God won't do what He created us to do, and we never ever can do what only God alone can do. God alone is sovereign.

So Habakkuk begins to get things back into perspective, realizing that only God is sovereign, that God is in control. This is very important, because God wants us to be obedient, and do exactly what He says. He alone is sovereign.

So then he humbles himself by saying, "Revive your work in the midst of the years." It is God's work. He is the Lord of revival, not us. He realizes that throughout the years God has done a great work in the lives of many other people. He comes to the realization that he's not the first person who has experienced violence in his community. He's not the first person who has experienced heartache, pain, and sorrow. He realizes now that as God has delivered people in the past, now God can revive His work in the midst of years. If God did it before, He can do it again because He has all power. He is the Lord of revival. God and God alone is sovereign.

The Sovereign Source of Revival

So he says, "In the midst of years, make known, in wrath remember mercy." So he understands that there are many things that God is angry about, many things that he did not do. Likewise, there are things that we may not have done and places we should not have been. But he knows that God is the one, that He is the ultimate sovereign source of revival. He is the eternal revivalist; He is the Lord of revival.

And look at how Habakkuk closes the book. He comes from a place of great doubt to this point in the 17th verse of the 3rd chapter: "Although the fig tree shall not blossom...." All right. "Although the fig tree shall not blossom," meaning, "Lord, if you don't answer my prayer the way that I want it to be answered...."

And then he goes on and says, "Neither shall the fruit be in the vines." Things may not work out the way that I want them to

110

work out. Then he says, "The labor of the olive shall fail, and the fields shall yield no meat, and the flocks shall be cut off from the fold, and there shall be no herd in the stalls; yet will I rejoice in the Lord."

Rejoice in the Lord of Revival

Now I just love that. Kind of sounds like Job, "Though he slay me, yet will I trust him." God didn't slay him, but it's just the fact that he would trust Him, even if he did. That brings beauty to that quotation.

And that's the way we have to be. If things don't go the way that I want them to go I'm still going to trust in the Lord, no matter what. I'm in this until I see Jesus face to face. And when I see Him face to face, hey! Then I'm in it even longer. I know that we're in it for eternity and eternity is forever. That's the bottom line.

And he says, "Yet I will rejoice, I will joy in the God of my salvation." I will joy in the Lord of revival, meaning that I realize that God is in control, that my life is in the hands of the Lord of revival. I have committed my way unto Him and He will direct my path. He will work it out. I don't know how He's going to work it out but I know that He will work it out. No matter what the trial is, the tribulation, the temptation, the heartache, the pain, peril, problem, or predicament. No matter what the situation is, God can solve it. He is the answer. It's not that He will bring the answer, but He is the answer, the Lord of revival.

Like Hinds' Feet

In essence he says, "The Lord God is my strength. He will make my feet like hinds' feet," like the little, small feet of deer. He says, "He will make my feet like hinds' feet, and He will make me. He will make me to walk upon high places." In other words, He's showing that there are some things that I cannot do. But I can pray. I can humble myself. I can seek His face. And

111

through His power I can turn from my wicked ways. The only reason I can do these things is through His power. Only He can exalt me. Only He can heal the land. Only He can help me and make me to walk upon high places, because I can't get up there by myself. And if I have feet that would stumble and fall, the Lord of revival can make my feet like hinds' feet in high places. When there are small ledges around the cliff, small ledges around the mountain that I could not climb myself, the Lord of revival will make my feet like hinds feet. He will help me to climb higher and higher to places we could never go.

There are things that you think you could never accomplish. You're trying to make them happen in the flesh, instead of birthing it in the spirit realm into the natural. But it's just not working. Well maybe that's not what God is calling you to make happen. He wants you to push and birth in the Holy Ghost. What He's calling you to make happen is just to pray, to seek His face and to wait on Him.

As we said before, just do that. Take solid godly action and then let the Lord of revival do what He knows how to do best. God will heal the land, He will heal those battered, broken, wounded places in your life. You must allow Him to lift you up where you belong, instead of trying to lift yourself up. If you focus on lifting up Jesus, He will meet your needs. What does the song say? "If I be lifted up, I'll draw all men unto Me." Let God do that.

So in closing, we cry out to God and say, "Help Lord, I need revival. This is my quest for spiritual renewal." And if we're honest with Him, God will do a work in our lives that we will never forget. He will manifest the fruit of those people who were touched through our living testimony.

Reach out to God and ask Him to touch you. Let the Lord of revival transform your life today.

Understanding the Meaning of Real Revival

Jesus Christ, the Lord of revival has given me, through the power of the Holy Spirit, three definitions of what revival is. In order to talk about the Lord of revival, in order to deal with the quest for spiritual renewal, we must understand what revival is. The Lord of revival, Jesus Christ, through the Holy Spirit, gave me the following definitions by laying them on my heart.

Firstly, revival is a spiritual quest. It is a constant journey to resurrect a dead, dormant and dull church into an organized group of captivating, committed and creative believers in Jesus Christ whose vibrant lives make a real difference in the real world that is full of real problems. Now, of course, this applies to the church at large, and this applies to people individually as well as collectively.

Secondly, the Lord of revival, gave me this definition, through the leading of the Holy Spirit. Revival is a divinely orchestrated and wondrous work of the Holy Spirit that convicts the church to rekindle the red hot flames of spiritual renewal and Godly integrity. This impacts the social, political and economic structures of society for the glory of God, even in the midst of great Christian persecution.

And thirdly, the prompting of the Holy Spirit laid this last definition on my heart to share with you. Real revival is an awesome move of God that clearly calls the church to complete repentance, more responsibility and renewed relationships with God. Thereby, bringing the fear of God Almighty back into the center of secular society.

A Major Move of God

To sum it up, revival is a major move of God. As I have stated before, It's what God has called us to do. Second Chronicles 7:14 brings it out the best: "If My people, which are called by My Name, shall humble themselves and pray and seek My face, and turn from their wicked ways...." These are the types of things that God wants us to focus on. We are commanded by God to humble ourselves to pray, to seek His face and to turn from our wicked ways. He has empowered us by the Holy Spirit to do this. Only God can hear from heaven, forgive our sins and heal our land.

But the next part of that verse is only what God can do, and that brings real revival. He said that if you do all of these things, "Seek My face, humble yourself, turn from your wicked ways, then..." then if you meet these conditions, "then will I hear from heaven, then will I forgive your sin, and then will I heal your land."

God wants us to seek Him. He wants us to cry out to Him, to pray, to turn from our wicked ways. He wants to bring the *then* factor into our lives. "The Lord of revival wants to bring the *then* factor, the factor in which we meet the conditions, in which He can step in and intervene in our lives, and bring forth a revival so we'll reap a great harvest of souls.

The Call To Commitment - Are You Ready for the Real Revival Revolution?

The Bible says "The harvest is ripe, but the laborers are few." God is calling us to commitment. This prayer that Habakkuk prays, "Lord revive thy work in the midst of the years," is the cry of Christian commitment. It's a burden cry of spiritual commitment. The fact that he has come out of the midst of his doubt, and now is asking God to send revival, shows spiritual growth. The fact that you are interested in this subject shows some interest in growing spiritually.

"God can do exceedingly, abundantly, above all that we ask or think." The Lord of revival wants to revolutionize your life. The Lord of revival wants to revolutionize your home. The Lord of revival wants to revolutionize your financial planning. The Lord of revival wants to revolutionize your relationships. The Lord of revival wants to revolutionize your mind, that it might be renewed by the power of His Word.

"Be not conformed to this world, but be transformed by the renewing of your mind." That's what the quest for spiritual renewal is all about. Responsively, your mind is transformed by ideas and concepts, through the vision of victory that God has for you.

Catch that vision of victory and never give up. Don't try to grab the vision that Madison Avenue, gangs, drug addicts, or a bully give you. Neither should you embrace the vision that would come through those who want to cause peer pressure and say, "Do it my way." But get God's vision for your life! Believe in that vision so deeply that your mind is transformed, renewed, revived and rejuvenated through the power of God's Word.

God's Word is eternal truth. God is the eternal revivalist. He wants to revolutionize your very being. The Word says, "In Him we live, and in Him we move, and in Him we have our being." He created you, He created me, He knows everything that there is to know about us. There is no one better to bring the revival, to bring the revolution, to bring the transformation that we need so desperately. Run for it. Don't let it go. Don't let go of the Lord of revival.

Jesus Christ, the Omnipotent, the Omniscient, and the Omnipresent Revivalist

There is no drug that is more powerful or potent than the Lord of revival. He is omnipotent, He is omniscient and He is the omnipresent revivalist. He's everywhere at the same time. If you are shooting up crack, He's there. If you're sniffing cocaine, He's there. If you're taking heroin, drinking liquor, wine and beer, or if you're strung out on drugs, He's still there. He's there to save. He's there to deliver, and He's there to restore and to revive your soul.

The Bible says that He, the Lord of revival, is married to the backslider. The Lord of revival cares about your soul. The Lord of revival cares about the prison bars that you are behind. The

Lord of revival cares about the bondage that you're in. The Lord of revival wants to bring inner healing to your life. He wants to revive His works in the midst of the years in your life, and He can do it like no one else can, because He is the Lord of revival.

The Spirit of the Lord gave me a song recently that exemplifies and summarizes the message that He gave to Habakkuk. It's also the message that He's giving to His church today. The song is called "Revive Thy Works." It says: "Oh Lord, revive thy works in the midst of the years; Lord revive us, please renew my spirit with brokeness and tears; Lord revive us. Oh Lord, revive my soul. Please cleanse and make me whole. Revive thy works, Lord, in the midst of the years. My burdened soul needs revival, revive thy work, Lord.

Jesus Christ is the omnipotent, the omniscient, the omnipresent revivalist. Jesus Christ, the Lord of revival, wants to run a revival service in your life. If you allow Him to come in and take control, not only as your Savior, but as the Lord of your life, the Lord of your personal and corporate revival, you will never be the same again.

The Bottom Line of Real Revival

Please remember that the bottom line of real revival is that the Lord of revival, Jesus Christ, is sovereign. If we disobey Him, we will be like a disobedient tribe of Judah in the book of Habakkuk that was called to lead in praise, but was punished for not doing in word and deed what God empowered them to do. Therefore, God allowed punishment to come upon Judah through the Chaldeans (Babylonians).

Chapter 6

AFTER TWO DAYS HE WILL REVIVE US - GET READY TO RISE AGAIN

Hosea - a Minor Prophet with a Major Message

Dear Reader, draw your attention to the book of Hosea. Hosea is one of the Minor Prophets in the Old Testament. He was one of the Minor Prophets who had a ministry to the Northern Kingdom in Israel. The date of his writing was between 1715 and 1710 BC, (before Christ). The book of Hosea is filled with beautiful language.

Hosea was a prophet who truly could relate to the plight of Israel more than any of the other prophets. He had a firm grasp and a deeper understanding of the sinful condition of Israel. Because, there were some things that God required of him that went above and beyond the normal call of duty. There were situations that effected his everyday life that most Christians would not put up with. But God called Hosea to live with this situation, with this cross, with this burden.

The Bible tells us in Hosea, the 1st chapter and the 2nd verse, "And the Lord said to Hosea, Take unto thee a wife of whoredoms and children of whoredoms; for the land hath committed great whoredom, departing from the Lord."

Married to a Prostitute

God called the prophet Hosea to marry a woman of ill repute. God called the prophet Hosea to marry a woman of the night, a woman of great compromise.

One might ask, "Why would the Lord allow this and ordain this? Why was it predestined to occur?"

The verse clearly lets us know that not only was God calling Hosea to marry this woman, but this woman was very much like Israel whose God, "Ish," was their husband. And they were in adultery against God. They were serving and worshipping idols. God wants our undivided attention. The Bible says that "Our God is a jealous God." One of God's names is "jealous". There is something that He sees in us, because He has created us.

He knows that the best thing for us is to serve Him all the days of our life. God called Hosea into this relationship and Hosea's name means salvation. God wanted to bring salvation into this woman's life. Equally important, God wanted to bring the message of salvation more clearly to the children of Israel.

A Living Sermon

So Hosea was a living testimony. He was a walking and talking sermon. He lived out the text through his actions. Just think if God asked you to do something that you did not really want to be bothered with. Something that you did not want to accept or be associated with, but yet God would say, "I want you to go on and do My will."

God is aware of the sinful condition of many. And the commitment of Hosea to his wife, Gomer, is an example of God's love, unconditional love, for His children. God loved Israel so much that even in the midst of her backsliding ways, He wanted to give them a second, and a third, and a fourth, and a fifth chance. But they did not want to listen to the Word of the Lord.

What's in a Name?

In the midst of this relationship, this woman goes out during the late hours of the night. Hosea and Gomer had three children. Their children each had a name that clearly represent God's judgment upon the children of Israel.

The first child born from this marriage was named Jezreel which means "God scatters". God was still trying to speak to

119

Israel. God allowed Hosea to be in this marriage with this woman, a woman who one might consider to be a woman of ill repute. God was trying to give Israel a chance, but they didn't want to listen, so God was beginning to scatter and divide them, because they would not seek His face. If we don't seek the face of God, God will scatter us. He will allow us to become divided, and go up in our own ways, because we're not seeking His ways.

Then they had another child named Loruhamah, meaning "not hidden." God loved them, but there came a point where He would have no pity upon them. He had no pity because their hearts became hard to God. They became like fallow ground, not broken up. It was so hard you could not plant anything. You could not get any seed into that ground. You could not get any Word in that ground, because it was so hard it would not accept the seed of God's Word and God's love.

Then they had a third child, Loammi, meaning "not my people." Israel was the chosen people of God, to a point. Nevertheless, they constantly resisted the Lord. Just as Gomer, Hosea's wife, resisted his love, and his support, and his encouragement. She went out and slept with other men. In the same way Israel resisted the love, the support, the passion and the care of God.

In this context we turn to the 6th chapter, realizing that already in the 4th chapter and the 6th verse God is so angry He says that "My people are destroyed for a lack of knowledge, because they have rejected knowledge, and I will also reject these that thou shalt be no priest to Me. Seeing thou hast forgotten the law of thy God, I will also forget thy children."

They rejected God, they rejected His message, just as Gomer had rejected the love of her husband, and went on to find many other lovers in the midnight hours.

Chapter 6 presents a peculiar set of scriptures. These three verses have been argued by theologians, and they have wondered, is this the prophet speaking? Or, is this the people speaking?

As I began to pray and meditate on it, the Spirit of God gave me an answer. Not only are these verses an example of the prophet writing and the people speaking, but also an example of God speaking. In this particular set of verses, there are three levels of rules, three dimensions of the same truth that is included in these three verses of scripture.

Returning to the Lord of Revival

It says, "Come and let us return unto the Lord, for he hath torn...." Listen to the language, church: "and He will heal us." He has torn us and He will heal us; He has smitten us, and He will bind us." Listen to that language. You don't hear many sermons like that.

"After two days will He revive us; and in the third day will He raise us up, and we shall live in His sight. Then shall we know, if we follow to know the Lord; His going forth is prepared as the morning; and He shall come unto us as the rain, as the latter and the former rain unto the earth."

Turn to your neighbor and say, "After two days He will revive us." That's the message here. After two days He will revive us.

Originally these were letters and messages written by prophets. There were no chapters or verses originally. But for the benefit of our understanding many years later, chapters and verses were put in so we could get a clear understanding of the subject matter. Originally there were no chapters and verses, that it was just a block of scripture, just a message from the Lord, a book without any chapters or any particular verses numbered. Then you'll begin to understand that what goes on in the 5th chapter has relevance to what's going on in the 6th chapter.

So in 5:15 it says, and remember, God is speaking: "I will go and return to My place, till they acknowledge their offense, and seek My face in their affliction, and they will seek Me early."

So in other words, God is saying, "They're going to seek me early."

In the 6th chapter, God is saying what they will say: "This is what they're going to say." Now they have said it, but God is saying, "This is exactly what they're going to say. Come and let us return unto the Lord; for He hath torn, and He will heal us; He hath smitten, and He will bind up. After two days He will revive us; in the third day He will raise us up, and we shall live in His sight."

Brought Out of Slavery

First of all, God prophesied that the children of Israel would say this. But remember, God was talking about the children of Israel being in their offense.

Just like Gomer, Hosea's wife, this prostitute was an offense in the relationship. The marriage bed was defiled. It was a sin against God, but God allowed Hosea to be in that situation, to be a living sermon of His love and His commitment to Israel. In like manner, Hosea would not leave Gomer, even when she was sold into slavery, because of her prostitution. Regardless, he was willing to go in and buy her back out of slavery because of the love that he had for her. It wasn't so much a miracle what he did for her, because he was supposed to care for her. But it was a miracle of the love that he had for her, being such a great prophet of God.

God wants us to love everybody, no matter what their situation or their predicament might be. But God says that this is what they're going to say. And what God says lets us know that this has some meaning. But when the children of Israel say it, they're saying it in the sense of, "Okay, we know that we're in sin. Come, let us return unto the Lord, and after two or three days He's going to revive us. We'll sin today, and He'll forgive us tomorrow."

Out of insincerity the children of Israel said it. For them it wasn't true repentance. Because God said it first, they would say it. The scripture has a deeper meaning. The first meaning of this scripture, of course, goes back to the fact that the children of Israel were saying that, "Okay, in two days He's going to revive us. We're going to repent and backslide and He'll forgive us of our sin. It wasn't genuine repentance. They were just trying to say, "Okay, we'll just be business as usual afterwards. We ask God to forgive us. We'll get up off our knees. In two or three days, everything is going to be fine. Then we'll just go back to business as usual."

After Two Days

God did not appreciate their insincerity. That is the first level of meaning of that scripture, but yet there is a deeper meaning. When you look at that second verse, it says, "After two days will He revive us."

The children of Israel didn't realize when they were saying this that during Christ earthly ministry these words would come to pass. First, they crucified Him on Calvary's cross. Then He lay in the tomb two complete days. But early that Sunday morning, God revived His body and raised Him up. Victoriously, Jesus rose from the dead with all power in His hands.

See, the children of Israel were speaking the truth but they were living a lie. Then there are a lot of folk who can speak the truth, preach the truth, sing the truth, talk about the truth, but yet are living a lie.

God says, "Even in the midst of them living a lie, I'm going to take the truth and I'm going to change lives." Even if Israel doesn't repent, and they didn't repent, Israel really didn't become a formal nation till 1948. They never repented. They heard all of the prophets that we hear about in the Old Testament, but they never repented the way that God wanted them to repent. That's the reason why the prophets are so important, because now their messages apply to us today.

We Were Raised Up with Christ

So we see the first level of meaning, and what was going on in the past. Now let's examine the second level of meaning. The essence of this prophecy is evident in the resurrection of Jesus Christ. It says, "After two days," meaning on the third day He will revive us, and then the third day He will raise us up. But that is strange, because it didn't say that it would raise Him up, but that it would raise us up.

But I want you to know something. When Jesus rose from the grave, we got up with Him. Every problem, every heartache, every pain, every situation, every heart break, every hurt, every situation, Jesus took with Him, and gave us the victory. That scripture, "Oh death where is thy sting," that comes out of the book of Hosea. Hosea was the one who originated that saying. God gave it to him first. And the apostle Paul took it; that was actually a spin off of what God had given Hosea.

And there are many scriptures that you'll read in the book of Hosea that you'll hear Jesus preaching from. You'll hear the apostle Paul and Peter, and their spin on what God has already said through the prophet Hosea. Hosea had a fine grasp of what was going on because God allowed him to be in a marriage that was a mess. But out of that mess God made a miracle. "In two days… He will revive us."

Let's look at 1st Corinthians 15:4. I want to show you that this scripture was fulfilled. First Corinthians 15:4 says, "He was buried, and then He rose again the third day, according to the scriptures." After two days He revived us.

The New Millennium - The Third Day

After the start of the 21st Century, there is a third level of understanding and revelation concerning this scripture. Concerning this word from God Israel just took it nonchalantly, just playing around and not genuinely repenting, not realizing that these were words or things from God that would have impact, even up until today.

In the new millennium, there is another aspect of scripture that the church, prior to now, could never fathom. The scripture says that a thousand years is as one day in the sight of the Lord. And the calendar that we go by in the United States and throughout most of the world, is based upon Christianity—A.D., and B.D., all of the months, the Christmas season, and Easter. All of these things are based on the Christian calendar.

So in the year 2001, we ended the second millennium, going into the third millennium and went into the third day. And it says that "after two days, He will revive us." After two days, He will revive us. After two days is the third day.

No Man Knows the Day or the Hour

Now somebody might say, "Well, Rev. Mackey, are you saying that after two days the rapture is going to occur?"

The Bible says, "No man knows the day nor the hour." And this scripture definitely deals with days, so that's not the real point of this scripture.

When it says that He will raise us up, it's talking about what God was trying to get across to Israel, but they didn't accept. God allowed them to fall because they did not accept His Word, and it also talks about what Christ has provided for us through the resurrection on the third day.

But then it also talks about what God wants to do in the church. In the first millennium, the church was strong. They laid hands on the sick, they raised the dead, they went forth, the Bible was written and published, and distributed all throughout the earth and Christianity grew to great proportions.

And in the second millennium, Christianity did spread, but towards the end of the millennium, Christianity began to lose its integrity. The world began to lose respect for the preachers of the gospel. And the world began to lose respect for the church. The new age movement began to rise. People began to say, "God is the sun," and "God is in the moon." We can listen to, not just our messages or sermons, but all the motivational messages, and

125

motivational music. It doesn't have to have the name Jesus in it. As long as it reflects the ideology that God is a higher power, a supreme being or that He might be a he, she or it, some people are satisfied. As long as this occurs, we are constantly moving away from God.

A Time of Integrity for the Church

God is saying that in spite of all of that, in spite of the backslidden state of preachers and teachers and churches, in spite of every scandal that's going on in the third day I will raise them up. "After two days I will revive them."

We're coming into a time of integrity for the church. We're coming into a time in which the church must carry herself in a different manner. We must carry ourselves with excellence and realize the power of the message that we proclaim, knowing that we have the only message that can save the masses. We have the only message that can turn the mess around. We have the only message that can bring healing to the land. The Word says, "If My people, which are called by My Name, shall humble themselves and pray, and seek My face, and turn from their wicked ways, then, and only then will I hear from heaven and heal, forgive their sins and heal their land."

Judgment Begins at the House of God

Healing is not going to happen in the White House. Healing is not going to happen in the Congress. Healing is not going to happen in the town hall, or at the county executive's office. Healing is not going to happen in any of those places, but it's going to have to come through the church of God, seeking the face of God. Because the Bible says, "Judgment begins at the house of God," then it goes to the world.

And as long as governmental leaders, as long as people in the community see the church live any old way, then they feel it's all right for them to live any old way. Even if they don't want to admit that we're the head and not the tail, above and not beneath, they know deep in their spirit that God has placed us here to be the salt of the earth. We're the thing that keeps us together. Rev. Dr. A.R. Bernard states in his message "The Culture of Christianity" that, "As Christians, we must no longer allow ourselves to be defined as a religion. We're a culture. A religion is a set of beliefs and practices that are used only at certain times - in many cases, just once a week. But a culture is a way of life that directs our words and conduct everyday." [1]

So the Bible says that when we are raptured, the whole thing is going to fall apart. If you think you've got tribulation, it's nothing now. Satan is going to be unloosed in full fury. And he's just waiting around, he's just ready, but he can't do what he really wants to do. You think things are bad? They aren't bad until we are out of here. Once we're out of here all hell is going to break loose.

But it says, "In the third day He will revive us." He will bring us into a new ministry of integrity. We will have to carry ourselves in a different manner. We're going to have to wait because the real fulfillment of this is in the resurrection of Jesus Christ. If we realize that in Jesus rising from the dead, we have also raised up, that He has also allowed us to go forth in the ministry that God has called us to. Whether that ministry is singing, preaching or teaching, whether it's in government within the church, the ministry of helps or whatever it might be, God wants you to excel and be excellent in that. Amen. I agree with the statement of Winkie Pratney: "Revival is more than big meetings, religious excitement, a quickening of the saints, being filled with the Holy Spirit, or great harvest of souls. One may have one or all or these without revival."[2]

If We Follow To Know the Lord of Revival

The next verse explains and breaks it down, for it says, "Then shall we know if we follow to know the Lord," meaning that this prophecy will be fulfilled in your life if you follow to know. If you are persistent, if you follow up, if you're consistent you shall know.

No, it won't happen in your life if you don't follow. It won't happen in your life if you're not consistent, but "You shall know if you follow to know."

So if we follow up, it will happen in our life, and it says, "His going forth is prepared as the morning. And He shall come as the rain." The rain is representative of the Holy Spirit. It says, "As the latter rain and the former rain in the earth." The former rain was the breaking of up the fallow ground, and getting ready to plant, getting ready to toil the ground at that time. That's the former rain, when they're doing the planting.

The latter rain is rain that comes during the age of the church, during the time of the harvest, during the time of the fullness of the prophecy being fulfilled. We're the only part of the church that has lived in the time where this prophecy can be fulfilled in its fullness. There is no other part of the church that has been alive to see this scripture fulfilled in its fullness. But we did. We're right there, and we have to say, "Here I am Lord, send me." Raise that anointing in me that will transform lives. People are hurting all over. There is something that God wants to do to the people. God has blessed you with knowledge, skills and education. He has given you these blessings for a reason. He wants you to use them for the kingdom of God.

"Revive me, Lord, by your Spirit! Bring real revival. Bring spiritual renewal into my life. Bring integrity into my life. Make me a trustworthy person! Help me, Lord God, to live right when nobody is looking. Help me to live right when only you are there. Help me to live right regardless if someone is looking. Help me to stay on the straight and narrow path. Lord, send the revival, and let it begin in me."

I lift up my hands and give God the praise. Thank you, Jesus.

PART THREE:

THE REVIVAL EXPERIENCE

Chapter 7

INTERVIEWS CONCERNING REVIVAL- HELPING REAL PEOPLE WITH REAL PROBLEMS FULFILL THEIR DESTINY

In our discussion of Real Revival, A sovereign Move of God, we've already learned about Ezra. His name means "help". It foreshadows the sovereign help of a sovereign God that we receive through the comfort of the Holy Spirit and the fact that Jesus is our help.

Also, we have learned about Habakkuk through his prayer, "Revive thy works in the midst of the years." And the Psalmist prayed, "Wilt thou revive us?"

But in practical terms, what does revival mean in our everyday lives? What does it mean when we go through painful and hurtful situations? I'm sitting today with Sister Debbie Jackson Woodside. Debbie is the head of Encourage Yourself Ministries, a worldwide ministry that encourages people all across the world with the gospel of our Lord and Savior Jesus Christ.

Debbie is a single parent, and a proud new homeowner who believes that the experience of purchasing a home was a blessing from God. As a Christian woman and the head of a ministry, Debbie lives a life that exemplifies Christ. Her unconditional love for people has catapulted her ministry beyond expectations, not through words, but through actions. I truly believe that her experience best exemplifies what we're trying to get across in this book. We need genuine Christians who stand on the Word of God. We need realistic believers who do not compromise

God's Word, or use cheap grace, but rather who flow in the grace of God which ushers us into holiness. And it's not because we're afraid of going to hell, but because we love God.

I want Debbie to expound on her experience of purchasing a home, including some of the trials and tribulations that she has gone through. I believe readers will be encouraged in every aspect of their lives. The quest for spiritual renewal goes beyond getting a spiritual message. It gets on the inside of us and brings integrity into every aspect of our lives. Yes, it is important for revival to start in the church. We must experience a personal revival as well.

Bob Carlisle wrote the song, "I Need a One-Man Revival." Debbie didn't experience a one-man revival, but she experienced a one-woman revival. We want her to address that. I believe her experience will touch the hearts of readers.

Revival Fire that Activates Faith By Debbie Jackson Woodside

Thank you, Rev. Mackey. When I think of revival, I think of something dead that has been brought back to life. You can define it in a lot of ways. When it seems like you're in a barren land where there is no growth, no fruit, no fruition, and it seems like the ground is dead, you can't use that ground to plant or to harvest anything. Revival is like breathing life into something, or restoring life into something once dead.

God breathed the breath of life into my situation. At one time my two daughters and myself were looking for a place to live. Society tells you that based on income and single parent status, you cannot obtain things that will increase your standard of living--especially a household that does not have an overly generous cash flow. We all know that with God all things are possible. He brought it to pass. God made it happen.

Sometimes we think we no longer have certain abilities or gifts. Sometimes we experience a loss of passion in our lives because of trials and tribulations. The enemy wants us to believe

131

that we've lost everything, that we cannot regain or overcome dilemmas. But we can.

I'm not going to say that it's easy. The physical eye captures a situation that looks dismal and bleak, with no cause for hope. You have to look with the eye of faith that says, "I can make it, regardless of how dark the situation maybe." We know that God can do anything but fail.

It's like Ezekiel in the valley of dry bones. When you walk into that valley, all you see is death. You don't see any life, and you don't see how life can exist in a barren land. But as the prophet began to speak words of life to the dry bones, flesh came upon the bones and the bones experienced a revival. In like manner, we must speak life into our personal situation; we must fan the flames of revival for ourselves. Ezekiel's words of faith brought about realization of those bones. Because of the work of the Holy Spirit these bones shall live.

I would like everyone to know that revival is an important part of your life. It's a daily thing. Revival is not a weekly, monthly or a once-a-year event. It can be a daily event, because for each day that you've gone through something, or have dealt with something, or something has tried to hinder you, the Lord will revive your spirit. You have to encourage, revive and stimulate those dead areas in your life so that you can move on.

Rev. Arthur Mackey is very inspirational. He and his wife, Brenda, are truly people of God and God is breathing revival constantly within their lives. For instance, God has revived my sister to the point where she saw that she could go forth and own her own business. So she began to walk by faith. As a result, she has purchased several things to start her own business.

There was a time when my sister may have thought, "Well no, I can't do this. It's too time consuming," or, "I have too many responsibilities," or, "I don't have the time to research the possibilities." But God has put her in a position where she is now able to re-think the possibilities.

So in that area she thought was dormant she's now creative, able to see the fruitful work of God in her life. She's been

132

revived. I must also mention Arthur Mackey, Jr. Rev. Mackey is an anointed gospel preacher who walks by faith and exemplifies Christ in his everyday life. It's evident that God has blessed Rev. Mackey and his wife. Great blessings await those who step out on faith. I know that some areas in your lives might be lacking. But God takes you and plants you there, to make you see that yes, that area of your life can be revived, it can be restored.

Courage That Produces Victorious Results

We need to continually revive ourselves by saying, "Hey, I'm waking up this morning. I wasn't able to take care of those two files that were on my desk at work, but today I'm going to complete those two files, and I'm going to handle the situation."

You may be a supervisor or a manager. Unfortunately you may be saying that you have to tell certain people that you're going to fire them, yet you don't see how you can do it. But God gives you a revival, He gives you the courage to know that you can do it.

I really feel good in my spirit knowing that there was a time when people thought that I could not obtain what I have obtained. It was not of my goodness; it was of God. He motivated me and the love that I have for God. See, when you love someone, you see a lot of good things in them. Sometimes you see a lot of good things in them that they don't see themselves.

Because I love God, and because I believe in God, His Word tells me that I can do all things through Christ who strengthens me; I am more than a conqueror. Each time I read it, I am revived, strengthened by the Word. When I look around with my physical eye, the enemy says, "Are you kidding me? There's no way you can accomplish what you want to accomplish because you're here."

So I just want to say in closing, be encouraged. Do not look at where you presently are. That is not always the end or the complete vision. Look towards God. Read His Word. He will encourage you more than you know. You can succeed.

The Word "revival" means to me, bring back from the dead. Bring back from the darkness. Bring back from all the impossibilities. When man says you can't, God said yes, you can. Keep the faith because God can bring restoration and renewal to those dead areas in your life. I praise God for this time. Amen.

#

I want to thank Sister Debbie Woodside, head of Encourage Yourself Ministries, for sharing her viewpoints on revival, and breaking it down in practical terms of what revival can mean in everyday life.

As I said before, the example of her being a single parent, a Christian woman and a home owner, is an example that truly exemplifies what revival is all about. Revival is not just something that we preach in our churches. It's something that we experience in our lives, because God doesn't dwell in four walls. He dwells in the hearts of men and women, boys and girls, throughout this world.

When we make a statement such as "Help, We Need Revival," in essence we're making a crystal clear admission to God that He is my help. He is the source of my strength, the keeper of my soul. The Holy Spirit is called alongside to help me as my comforter. And without the presence of the Holy Spirit, without the Spirit of Christ, without the omnipotent presence of God, I cannot experience revival.

When we use the word "help," we're actually referring to the help that the Holy Spirit provides.

I'm sitting here today with Cousin Joann. She's going to talk to us about revival. She's going to share some of her experiences. In the midst of it, God has spoken to her. She will share how she has experienced revival in terms of her faith and personal relationship with God, how she was strengthened, redeveloped, re-shaped and molded.

So right now we're going to turn it over to Joann, she will share with us her own revival and how God has spoken to her in the midst of life's harshest storms.

When Storms Arise, Focus on the Lord of Revival By Joann Cornick

It's hard to find a place to start, but you have to start somewhere. Let me go back a few years. Life was good, considering my age. At 59, my life was moving along with ups and downs, highs and lows. I'd had good times and sad times, but on average I've had ordinary times.

And then, all of a sudden, last year was the worst year of my life. I believed in God. I belonged to a certain faith and I went to church. I didn't go every Sunday, but I believed in God.

At any rate, last year all of a sudden my life took a turn for the worst. My parents died a year apart. I was extremely close to both of them. They were my mentors, my advisors. I had the greatest of respect for both of them. My dad died from a short term illness, and my mother died of colon cancer. That just absolutely devastated me.

During that time there were two or three other family members close to me who died. So I spent a whole year focusing on death and dying, nothing else but death and dying. I lived and functioned, but my whole emphasis was centered on my sorrow.

Just before that, my husband and I had joined a church together. We both were of different religions, but we joined a church together. We were very happy to begin to learn the Bible. At our ages, we looked to see what life is really about. Having God is a very important part of our lives.

But, as all these things happened, life seemed to become bleak. When my mother and father died, everything had started happening to me. And then in conjunction with that, I became

135

ill. Three months after my mother died I had a coronary--a blockage in the heart. I was in the hospital twice and had surgery with the angioplasty.

Bed-ridden, sick, devastated, with no parents, I was as low as the human spirit could possibly go. But I got a little bit better, yet still discouraged, still depressed, still sad, and still down.

Endurance Pleases God

At the end of that year, while my husband and I were out for the afternoon, our house was robbed! I mean, the house was totally trashed--everything was gone or thrown all over the place. Many of our things were stolen.

Right in the midst of all that, when my husband and I came in the house, and we saw that somebody had been in there, I looked up to the ceiling, and I said, "What does God want?"

At that point, my husband and I got into an argument. He thought that I was losing my faith, turning against God. And I said to him, "Richard, I'm not turning against God." I said, "He understands me. I'm asking Him a question, what does He want from me?"

I'd been a good person, I'd been a decent person. Now all of this was happening to me. What could be worse? All I'm asking Him is what does He want me to do?

So my husband just looked at me in shock. He knows more about the Bible and understands more than I do, so he said, "Joann, you have to remember the story of Job. That man lost everything. He lost his health, he lost his children, and even his wife tried to turn him against God. And Job said, 'No, I will be a believer.'"

Give God the Praise

So, though this bad thing happened to me, God was working in my life. Two days later I said to my husband, "Richard, guess what! God has given me the answer. He wants me to be closer to

Him." That was so important. It was a revelation to me. Yes, bad things happened and it was a whole bad year for me.

People resist change. Nobody wants change. I started reading the Bible when my husband and I joined the church. I wanted to have God in my life more, but never really sought Him. Wanting something and doing it became my quest night and day.

Evidently this had to happen to me. I had to be hit over the head in order for me to crank up.

I'd like to add to that I thought about a conversation I had with my cousin, Arthur, the family's minister and spiritual counselor. He said, "When you're going through trials and tribulations you must give God praise." Let me tell you, I never ever forgot those pearls of wisdom.

Another thing comes to mind: Some years ago in Florida, I saw on television the devastation from floods and hurricanes. I saw how people's houses and businesses were all in splinters no bigger than toothpicks. They showed this devastation for a whole week on television. And then that Sunday in church blacks, whites and people of all colors were united. I'm sure that was because of the devastation. They would not speak otherwise. They were all sitting in the same church, and they were all singing, "How Great Thou Art." Absolutely powerful and overwhelming. I just loved it. I never forgot that.

Triumphant Over Trials

So all I can say about my own testimony is that God is good. He is powerful and He allows things. He doesn't do anything bad because He is all good, and all merciful. Things will happen in your life to really show you that God is in your corner. He's for you, but He showed me that I have to love Him. I'm reading the Bible now. I'm going to church more. I am interested in learning about God, and the love of the Lord. I hope this will help someone. Thank you very much.

Arthur L. Mackey, Jr.

#

Revival Works Wonders

Thank you, Joann. We're talking about Revival. These testimonies reveal what revival is all about. God steps into a situation to give an answer in the midst of your storm, in the midst of your pain. There are a lot of people in the world today who are hurting, who are going through horrible situations. And they're crying out, "Help! I need revival."

And God, I believe, will bring revival to our lives personally and also to our churches corporately. But we have to be honest with Him. A lot of people are saying, "Well, you know there's a revival going on in this city, and in that city, but we don't need revival. We don't need to pray to God."

But I believe that we need to be honest with God. Even great religious leaders that I talk to and great spiritual leaders need personal revivals. Great singers, teachers, doctors, lawyers, people working in the community need revival. We see them in one category but God really sees their heart. God sees the hurt and the pain that they're going through. Many are crying out, "Help! I need revival."

I really believe what Joann has shared here will help people to experience revival in their lives. A lot of times when they're going through painful situations, people ask, "Where is God?" Or, "What am I doing wrong?"

I was sharing with Joann and with the church also that many times when we go through difficult situations we find Satan coming against us. That's a clear indication that we're doing something right. Satan will not come up against anyone that he does not see as a threat to his kingdom. But when you're coming closer to God, when you're seeking the Lord, which is one of the main key points to bring us into revival, the Bible says, "Seek ye first the kingdom of God, and all these things shall be added unto you."

When we begin to seek the face of God, Satan comes up against us the hardest because we become a threat to his kingdom. Through these types of conversations, he knows that other people will be blessed and other people will be encouraged. Other people are crying out, "Help! I need a touch from God," and, "Help! I need fresh fire from God. Help! I need revival."

We'll begin to experience that revival. Bob Carlisle has a song titled, "I need a one-man revival." Not only do we need a one man revival, in many cases we need also a one-woman revival, a one-son, a one-daughter revival, a revival for our whole family, a revival for our whole church. Revival is for the church. God wants to revive His churches, which in many cases are dead.

A New Perspective

But thank God, in many cases there is a new, fresh life coming to many of our churches. What Joann has shared represents that fresh life, that fresh fire, that fresh anointing that God is sending. Of course, it's not easy. Jesus never promised us a bed of roses. He never promised that everything would go the way we want, but He did say, "Lo, I will be with you always, even unto the end of the world."

He also said that, "I'll never leave you nor forsake you." So even in the midst of the storm, God is there still saying, "Peace be still." He is still giving a word of encouragement, still giving inner healing and substance that will help us make it through the struggles of life.

And I'm so glad to have my wife, Sister Brenda Jackson Mackey here with me. My wife is pregnant with our son, Jordan, at this moment. She will have insights to share concerning this at a later date.

Cousin Joann, thank you for sharing. Is there anything else you'd like to share?

Well, yes. I would just like to say that it amazes me how powerful God is. He does things in His own way and in His own time. As Arthur said, God tells us things, and He shows us all things. He showed me. He had to make it so that I would see the situation for myself. It is important to know that God is the most important being that will ever be in my life. I want the love of God. I want to get closer to Him and to learn more about Him.

It is just amazing how He gave me the answer to the question that I was asking Him, "Lord, what do you want? What else do you want from me? I'VE BEEN A GOOD PERSON ALL MY LIFE. How could you let all this stuff happen to me?" That was my question to Him.

We all need God in our lives, as a flower needs water. I thank God that at 59 years of age I'm beginning to see the light. I thank Him very much.

Thank you, Joann. I'm blessed by what Joann is sharing. I can imagine it is devastating for someone to lose their father first, then to lose their mother, then to go to the hospital and have heart surgery, and then go through hard experiences in life, not neglecting responsibilities on the job, and in the home, the children, with family and community. It's amazing to make it through the things that she has made it through, and still have a praise, still have a song. It's just a major encouragement.

And that's why we're saying, "Help! We need revival." We want to provide real life examples from the Bible. For instance, Ezra. You know, Ezra talked about a little reviving in our bondage. Now listen to the language of that, "a little reviving in our minds." Evidently Ezra knew that his people and himself were going through some pain. But he talked about a little reviving in the bondage.

Lord, Send Revival

One of the Psalms says, "Wilt thou revive us again?" Okay, so here we hear this cry, "Help! We need revival." They didn't use those exact words, but it boiled down to the same thing. Habakkuk put it this way, "Revive thy works in the midst of the years." So he understood that there comes a time when we need God to revive something in us. Only God can revive that which is dead or that which is dying.

Regardless of what you're going through, it's important to praise God. It is important because the enemy of the soul is just waiting for us to fail.

Rev. Charles G. Finney makes this point clear:

"The world is divided into two great political parties. One party chooses satan as the god of this world, yields obedience to his laws and is devoted to his interests. Selfishness is the law of his empire. The other party chooses the eternal God for its governor and consecrates all its interests to His service and glory. But changing parties, from satan's to God's, does not imply an alteration of the parts or powers of body or mind anymore than a change of mind with regard to the form or administration of a human government requires a physical change of mind or body. The act is accomplishment by choice alone by a change of heart."[1] I thank God for Joann's honesty. I pray that as people read this it will bless their hearts. We have a lot of liars in the church who say that they're not going through any problems, they're not going through any heartache, they're not going through any pain. But God is not a man that He should lie. So God is truthful, and when people are truthful, they're letting the Spirit of God shine and flow through them. And Joann has been very truthful, very transparent. She just poured out her heart. I know that this is going to be a blessing to somebody else who is going through some tragic situations. Thank you very much, Joann.

Chapter 8

THE BURDEN OF REVIVAL - HOW BAD DO YOU WANT IT?

Write, Read, and Run

We must *write* the vision, we must *read* the vision, and we must *run* with the vision. Write that down--write, read, and run. Those are the three things that God wants us to do with the vision of victory.

That's the Biblical principle of success for real revival to occur in our lives. For the burden of revival to flow and bring spiritual integrity to our lives, to write that vision down. We could write it down three times if we want, one for the Father, Son and Holy Ghost, but write that vision down, and then read that vision, and then after you read that vision, begin to run with that vision.

Don't give up on what God has showed you in the wee hours of the morning. Don't give up on what God has shown you in the midnight hour. If God has revealed that word to you, hold on to that vision. Never give up.

Verse 3 says, "For the vision is yet for an appointed time, but at the end it shall speak and not lie; though it tarry, wait for it, because it will surely come and not tarry."

Spiritual Renewal on Massive Terms

Now let's look at the 12th verse in that 2nd chapter of Habakkuk. It says, "Woe to him that buildeth a town with blood, and establisheth a city by iniquity." We want to deal with the violence. We want to deal with the hardships, and God gives us a vision in order to inspire us, to give us the right direction, to give us the right spirit as we deal with the problems of the day.

But then the scripture clearly says, "Woe onto that person that will try to build a town, will try to build a city, a state, a nation with blood, who will try to build a town, will try to build a city, will try to build a nation with iniquity, with sin." There is no way that we can bring transformation to Nigeria, to Africa, to America or this world by trying to do it with our own philosophy. "It's not by might, it's not by power, but it's by My Spirit, saith the Lord," that revival will occur.

But you see what God's plan is concerning the burden for revival? The purpose is to bring about spiritual renewal on massive terms. This is explained in the 14th verse of the 2nd chapter.

The Knowledge of the Glory of the Lord

The 14th verse says, "For the earth shall be filled with the knowledge of the glory of the Lord as the waters cover the sea." That's why God wants us to have a vision of victory, to deal with the violence. That's why God doesn't want us to be discouraged or to give up. That's the reason why He wants us to have a burden for revival, because this thing is much bigger than what we think. This thing is much bigger than Nigeria. It's much bigger than Africa, and it's much bigger than America and England. He wants this gospel to be spread throughout the world. He wants the knowledge of this good news, this burden for revival, to cover the earth as the waters cover the sea.

Dr. Duewell states that "God understands. God loves. God has provided an answer. Call it renewal, call it revival, call it refreshing, or call it whatever you will: God planned the ministry of the Holy Spirit to meet this great need of ours. We all repeatedly need God's reviving touch. But there are special times when the church needs revival in an unusually urgent way. I believe we need revival desperately today."[1]

How many of you want to be a part of that revival? How many of you want to see that revival occur in Nigeria, America, England, Japan and everywhere? If you want to be a messenger in that revival, if you want to be an ambassador in that revival, give God some praise as you read this book. Hallelujah.

We're talking about "The burden for revival." Say, "Here I am Lord, send me. I'll go where you want me to go, and I'll do what you want me to do, because I'm yours Lord, everything I am and everything I'm not. Try me now and see if I can be completely yours."

There's a song that says that you're the only Jesus that some will ever see; that you're the only Bible that some will ever read. If they don't see the love of Jesus through you, if they don't see the love of Jesus through me, then they may never come to know the Savior.

Real Revival vs. Counterfeit Revival

Go forth in the Name of Jesus and preach that Biblical principle of success that I am not ashamed of the gospel of Jesus Christ, for it is the power of God unto salvation. I tell it everywhere I go. I'll tell it on the mountain top. I'll tell it on the roof top. I'll tell it in the streets that He healed me. I'll tell them that He delivered me. I'll tell them that He picked me up out of the muck and the miry clay, and placed me upon a solid rock, and established my goings. The Lord of revival gave me a burden for lost souls, a burden for transformed lives. Shout and thank God for the burden of revival. Hallelujah.

Let's look at the second chapter and the 19th verse. It says: "Woe unto him that saith to the wood, Awake." For God's revival there is a counterfeit type that Satan has where folk are bowing down to idols, when God wants us to put down all of our idols.

"Woe unto him that saith to the wood, Awake; and to the dumb stone, Arise, it shall teach. Behold, it is laid over with gold and silver, and there is no breath in the midst of it." Amen.

Buddha is dead. Mohammed is dead. Whether or not they make idols to them doesn't matter, because Jesus is the only One who rose from the dead and lives in the hearts of believers of the church today. Jesus is alive and well.

The Lord Is In His Holy Temple

The 20th verse says, "But the Lord..." Hallelujah. Buddha is not in his temple; Mohammed is not in his temple; but it says "But the Lord is in His holy temple." The Bible says that we are the temple of God, that He dwells in us. It says, "Greater is He that is in me than he that is in the world." Hallelujah. "The greater One lives in me, but the Lord is in His holy temple, let all the earth keep silence before Him.

The Lord of revival is bringing forth the burden for revival in the midst of His church. He's indwelling us. He's filling us with His Spirit. He's telling all the earth to keep silence before Him, saying, "Just shut up and listen. Look what I'm doing through My children. Look what I'm doing through My church." Hallelujah.

Singing a Prayer

The 3rd chapter, first verse, says, "A prayer of Habakkuk the prophet upon Shigionoth." Shigionoth means "a sacred song." So Habakkuk was singing this prayer. It started off with this burden that he had about the violence. Then in the 2nd chapter it dealt with this vision of victory that God told him about. I like to call it a vision of victory for lost souls, for lasting change, for lives to be revolutionized with the power of the gospel of Jesus Christ.

Then in the 3rd chapter, God brings together the burden of revival. His prayer is, "Oh Lord, I have heard they speech." Lord, I've heard everything that you said, "and I was afraid." Sometimes when you hear words from God it can shake you up, because you know that there is an awesome responsibility. But if

God gives you an awesome responsibility, He will also empower you to do the work.

Remember That Time

"Revive thy work in the midst of the years, in the midst of the years make known; in wrath remember mercy."

Can you remember when you first gave your life to the Lord? Can you remember that day? Can you remember that hour? Can you remember the time when you got saved? If you can remember that time, I want you to quietly ask God to revive that work of the Holy Spirit in your life. As Christians, we must not lose our first love. We must develop a burden for revival. It is time to remove the blinders and realize that there is a real world that is hurting and desperately needs the love and compassion of Jesus.

The late Rev. Dr. Sandy F. Ray wrote in his book, "Journeying Through A Jungle," that, "One of the major problems of people is mental, moral, and spiritual blindness. The mission of the Christian church is to lift the blinders off the minds and souls of humanity."[2]

An Active Agent of Real Revival

God wants to revolutionize Africa, America, England, Mexico and all the nations of the world. But it will happen only with a burden for revival. Not just a burden that pastors have, not just a burden the deacons have, or trustees, but a burden that the people have for change to come about. Repeat after me: "Holy Spirit, breathe on me; Holy Spirit, breathe in me; Holy Spirit, breathe through me; use me, use me, use me as an agent of revival."

John Taylor of London, England, prayed this prayer while we were conducting revival meetings in Lagos, Nigeria. He prayed, "Father God, in the mighty Name of Jesus Christ of Nazareth, impart that burden for revival in their very spirit. Empower them with the Holy Ghost to go forth and do their work on your behalf. And Father, I thank you that from this day forward, they will not be the same again. And Father, we ask that by your Holy Spirit that anointing and the presence of God would permeate, and fill, and drench, and spill from one unto the other Lord. Also that spirit of love, the spirit of compassion, the spirit of grace, the spirit of truth and the spirit of life from one to the other Lord. Thank you, Lord. Thank you, Lord."

Pastor John Taylor ended his prayer with these words, "And we praise you for it in the mighty Name of Jesus. Touch them, Lord. Touch them right now. Hallelujah. Amen.

Say aloud, "Thank God I am an active agent of real revival. God has called me as His revivalist in my home. God has called me as a revivalist in my land. Everywhere that I go I am an active agent of revival. I am a representative of real revival. Use me for your service in Jesus' Name." Hallelujah.

A Minor Prophet with a Major Message

Habakkuk is called a minor prophet, but the only difference between the Minor Prophets and the Major Prophets is that the major prophets wrote longer books while the minor prophets wrote shorter books. A major prophet like Isaiah had 66 chapters; the book of Habakkuk has three chapters. He's called a minor prophet, but he has a major message. We want to deal with something that God said to Habakkuk, and we want to deal with what God is saying to the church today.

A Burden You Can See

Now let us look at this familiar passage from the perspective of the Burden for Revival. The book of Habakkuk starts off with these words, "The burden which Habakkuk the prophet did see." We have to be able to see some things, and we have to be able to hear some things in reference to hearing the book of Revelation, which says, "He that hath an ear let him hear what the Spirit says to the churches."

147

As well as hearing what the Spirit says to the churches, we must see what God is doing. We must see what He is trying to reveal to us, even in the midst of the toughest times of life, even in the midst of trials and tribulations, even in the midst of tests and temptations that we all experience.

Habakkuk saw a burden. Do you have a burden for lost souls? Do you have a burden because you've seen that Satan has stolen things from the kingdom of God. He's stolen somebody's mother, somebody's son, somebody's daughter and somebody's father. He's pulled them into his kingdom and has them on liquor and on drugs. He has them caught up in violence. He has them caught up in sexual promiscuity.

Is there a burden for lost souls? Well Habakkuk could relate to the burden that you have right here in Africa for lost souls. And Habakkuk expresses the burden that he had.

The 2nd verse of the 1st chapter reads, "Oh Lord, how long shall I cry and thou wilt not hear, even cry out unto thee of violence." So Habakkuk had a burden. He was crying out to God concerning the violence in his nation.

I come from New York, and I'm concerned about the violence that is going on in New York. I have a burden concerning the violence that is going on in my community. I'm burdened by the black-on-black crime, the hate crimes, racial tensions between blacks and whites, between Jews and blacks, and all of the hatred that is going on in the land. I have a burden to see this thing change in the Name of Jesus.

Concerned About the Violence

So Habakkuk was concerned about the violence, and our theme is that "The violent take it by force." But there is a violence that is of the kingdom of God. When we realize that Satan has gotten violent with us, then we should overcome him with the spirit of revival. We recognize that Satan has stolen our children in many cases, that he has stolen our family, that he has stolen our sons and our daughters and our friends to drugs, and to peer pressure.

Young people are dying, even before the time that God wants to call them home. They're wasting their lives on things that are ruining their very existence--hanging out with the wrong people, getting arrested and not always because they have done anything wrong themselves, but they were with the wrong crowd. Sometimes you could be with the wrong crowd, and somebody might have drugs or they might have a gun, and they end up in jail just because they're with the wrong crowd.

Habakkuk was concerned about these issues. He was concerned about the violence, about the problems that were plaguing his people. Against the violence that Satan brings, there is a violence that God brings. But the violence that God brings is a positive violence. In fact, the word that is used in the scripture is "vision".

So for the negative violence that Satan brought about in the lives of the folk that Habakkuk was praying for, God brought a positive thing, and He called it a vision, and let's look at the 2nd chapter and the 1st verse. It says, "I will stand upon my watch and set me upon the tower, and watch to see what He will say unto me, and what I shall answer when I am reproved."

Habakkuk was praying in the 1st chapter. In his prayers he was complaining to God about the violence. He was complaining to God about the problems. Many times we pray and ask God why. Sometimes we should ask God why, if our heart is right. If we ask Him, believe me, He will give us an answer. It may not be the answer that we want, but he will give us an answer.

God Speaks

So God speaks in the 2nd verse of the 2nd chapter: And the Lord answered me." You see, if we ask the Lord something, we've got to watch out, because the Lord will answer. The Lord gives His answer to the negative violence. The Lord shows us

149

how we can get violent as Christians in the right way, and how we can take it by force. He shows us exactly how to do it: "Write the vision and make it plain upon tables, that he may run that readeth it." So in other words, he says, "Write, read and run."

God wants us to write down the vision that He is showing unto us. God constantly shows us His vision that God is imparting to the congregation, a direction that He wants you to go, and an impact that He wants you to have in your community.

God hasn't raised you up in this community for nothing. God has raised you up so you can make a difference. You're the only Jesus that some will ever see. You're the only Bible that some will ever read. If you don't stand up for Jesus Christ, there are many who will never come to know the Lord as Savior.

Then the Word goes on and says, "Behold, his soul which is lifted up is not upright in him, but the just shall live by faith." If you want to get "violent" with Satan, the only way that Satan is going to respect you is if you live by faith. If you're playing around, and if you are straddling the fence, as the saying goes, Satan will say to you, "Hey, I know Jesus. I know Pastor Beardorf. But who are you?"

But if you are walking by faith, as the scripture says, "The just shall walk by faith," when Satan sees you, and you say, "In the Name of Jesus, Satan I rebuke you." You know what he's going to see? He's not just going to see you. He's going to see Jesus in you. He's going to run in the other direction.

There is power in the Name of Jesus. We're talking about the burden for revival. God showed Habakkuk how He deals with the violence. He gives us a vision. And He says, "I want you to take that vision. I want you to write it. I want you to read it and run with it, and get violent with the devil.

Run with it to your next door neighbor's house. Run with it to your sister. Run with it and share it with your brother. Run with it and share it with your cousins. Run with it and share it with your daughters. Run and share it with your sons. Run and share it with your parents. Run and share it with your girlfriend, with your boyfriends, with your enemies, and with everybody that you can.

God's vision can be fulfilled. I believe there's a real burden for revival to see lives changed. There are so many people who are bound to cursing, bound to lying, bound to stealing, bound to dope. They have no hope for living. Some are thinking about committing suicide. They're at the end of their rope and they don't want to go on at all. But we've got a message that can change their lives. It's the power of the gospel of Jesus Christ if we just share that one word with them--Jesus. Old Mohammed is dead. Buddha is dead. But Jesus is alive. Hallelujah. See, what God wants to do when we get the burden of revival and spread it. That's the reason why He wants us to write the vision, read it, and run with it. He wants us to have this burden of revival to deal with the violent by getting violent in the positive sense. Give Satan a black eye by kicking the devil's behind.

In the 2nd chapter, and the 14th verse it says, "For the earth shall be filled with the knowledge of the glory of the Lord, as the waters cover the sea." He wants us to have a burden for revival. He wants us to have a burden for lost souls, why? He wants us to have a burden for our families to be saved, why? He wants us to have a burden for our relatives to be saved, why? He wants us to have a burden to see our enemies saved, our neighborhood saved, why? "So the earth shall be filled with the knowledge of the glory of the Lord, as the waters cover the sea." That's God's vision, and that's the burden that He wants us to have. If you've got that burden to see God's Word be spread, as the waters cover the sea, in your community, just stand on your feet right now, and say, "Go, God." Come on, lift up your hands and just say, "Go, God!" Two thirds of God's name is "Go". Do it, God. Send the revival. Let the revival begin in me. Let the burden for gospel begin in me.

The Revival Is Here

This little light of mine, I'm going to let it shine. Everywhere I go, I'm going to let it shine. I'm going to let it shine all in my neighborhood.

Hallelujah.

Have Personal Relationship with the Lord of Revival

What does God want us to do? He said, "If My people, which are called by My Name shall humble themselves and pray, and seek My face, and turn from their wicked ways, then will I hear from heaven, then will I forgive their sins, and I will heal their land."

That's the type of stuff that God wants us to do. That's the type of stuff that God wants us to be about. That's the type of business God wants us to be about.

So the Word goes on, saying, "Revive thy work in the midst of the years." This is Habakkuk's prayer. This is his burden. "In the midst of the years make known, in wrath remember mercy."

Everyone can remember a time when God moved in your life. Whether it was God speaking to you, to your heart, or if God was speaking through your grandmother, or through a preacher. Remember a time when God was trying to deal with you, and you began to draw nigh to God. The Bible says, "If you draw nigh to God, He will draw nigh to you."

Remember that time when you were first saved? Remember that time when you first met the Lord? Remember the time when you first came to the altar? Remember that time when the anointing first came upon you?

That is a work of God that must be revived. In doing the work of the Lord, we must not fail to keep an outstanding relationship with the Lord of revival. We want to go forth and do the work of the Lord, but we want to have an intimate relationship, a passionate relationship with the Lord of revival.

And if we are honest, we would admit that we need revival in our lives. We're not as spiritual as we would make some think that we are. It's easy for us to come out to church and it's easy to put on the facade.

Many of us know when to lift up our hands and when to clap them, and when to dance, and when to shout. But God wants to do a work in our lives, and that's when we get serious about that, that's when we're getting violent with the devil. Because then the devil knows that this isn't just Christianity at church, this is Christianity at home. This is Christianity when nobody else is looking.

The Promise of Revival

I believe God is speaking to someone right now, He's speaking to hearts because there is a great work that God wants to do. Bishop Eddie Long states, "We can't let despair overwhelm us. After all, you can't resurrect something unless it's dead. If we didn't have problems, we wouldn't need revival. I am not excited about the problems we still face, but I am excited that God is acting to overcome them![18] That's the promise of revival. Not everybody wants it. Not everyone will greet it gladly. But God is saying, "Those of you who are fed up with going through the motions, I have a revival going on in which I'm giving life. You who are tired of not seeing anything, who know there's more, who want to turn and offer yourselves to me - those of you who want to be real with me, come on!" [3]

I want to close this particular chapter with the 17th verse through the 19th verse, "Although the fig tree shall not blossom...." Everything is not going to go our way. The Lord didn't promise us a bed of roses, but what He did say is that "I'll never leave you nor forsake you." What He did say is, "Lo, I'll be with you always, even unto the end of the age."

"Neither shall the fruit be in the vines, the labor of the olive shall fail, and the fields yield no meat; and the flock be cut off from the fold, and there be no herd in the stalls. Yet I will."

We've got to get to the point where we say, "Lord, everything may not be going the way that I want it to go. I don't have all of the financial resources that I would like to have, but I'm blessed. I don't have all the earthly possessions that I would like to have. I don't have the house, I don't have the car that I would like to drive, but yet, I will rejoice in the Lord." Why? "Because the Lord is my strength." When we praise God from the depths of our heart, God receives joy, God receives glory, God receives honor.

Don't Give Up

What does He do? He stands up from His chair in the portals of glory, at the throne, and He throws down strength, He sees that you're praising Him, sister. He sees that you're praising Him, brother. He sees that you're worshipping Him. He sees that you're worshipping Him. The heart of God gets joyful and He throws down some strength.

If you need some strength, if you've got that burden, but you need a little more strength to make it, just begin to worship the Lord. "Oh magnify the Lord with me, let us exalt, let us exalt, let us exalt His Name together." Say, "I will joy in the God of my salvation, the Lord God is my strength, the Lord God is my strength."

You've got a burden for revival, but God is our strength to allow us to get violent with the devil, and take it by force. He will give us the strength to see what the end is going to be, He'll give us the tenacity, He'll give us the endurance. Somebody felt like giving up, somebody felt like turning back, somebody wanted to throw in the towel, somebody contemplated suicide, someone was discouraged about a relationship, someone was discouraged about the baby, someone was discouraged about the bills, someone was discouraged because they couldn't pay the rent.

But God is your strength. He'll make a way where there is no way. Doors will close but He'll kick them down. He just wants you to worship Him. He just wants you to learn of Him. He just wants you to let Him bring the discipline and training into your life that He's calling for right now. Listen! Can you hear? Can you see it? The Lord is in His holy temple. Come on and praise Him. Come on and worship Him. Oh magnify, oh magnify the Lord. Let's get violent with the devil. Let's give him a black eye. The devil has stolen our families. He's stolen our fathers. He's stolen our sons and our daughters, but we're taking back the power by force.

Revival Fire Gets Results

My soul looks back and wonders how I got over to righteousness. He saved my soul. If He can save my soul, He can save my family. If He could save my soul, He can save my community. If He could save my dirty, ugly, sinsick soul, then He could save the world.

I'm going to write it in the midnight hour, in the early morning, at noon day--all day. I'm going to write the vision. I am going to read it. I'm going to read it in the morning. I'm going to read it at noon. I'm going to read it in the midnight hour. Not only that, I can feel the fire burning in my feet. I can feel the fire burning in my hands. I can feel the fire burning in my soul. I can feel the fire burning in my spirit. I can feel the fire of revival. I've got to run for Jesus! Take the baton and run for Jesus. "Go ye therefore into all the world, and preach the gospel of Jesus Christ."

"Lord, we thank you for your Word. We thank you for your presence in our hearts. We pray, Lord God, that this message might not be in vain, but that it would make a difference in the hearts and the lives of readers. We pray not only as hearers of the Word, but as doers, in Jesus Name."

There might be one who has heard the message and wants this fire. Ask yourself the question, If I died tonight, somebody pulled me over, mugged me, shot me in the head, stabbed me, would I make it in the kingdom? Would I make it to heaven?

Or would I lift up my head in hell? If you're not sure about the status of your soul, if you don't have a relationship with Jesus Christ, if you need the Savior, give your life to Him.

Thank you Jesus. Forgive me for the wrong I've done, Lord. Send a revival, and let it begin in me. Thank you Lord for what you've done. Thank you, Lord, for the fire. Thank you, Lord, for the Holy Ghost. Bless and strengthen me. Keep me in the hollow of your hand, in Jesus Name. Amen.

Chapter 9

GENUINE REVIVAL IN AFRICA- SPREADING LIKE WILDFIRE

Going Home to the Motherland

On Thursday, October 16th, 1997, my father, my mother and of course my lovely wife Brenda Jackson Mackey, and our daughter, Yolanda Alicia, took me to John F. Kennedy Airport in New York. I was filled with great anticipation because I was going to catch a flight to Ojokoro, Ghana, then to Lagos, Nigeria, my main destination.

I was going to Lagos to conduct a revival under the invitation of the Rev. Dr. Chris Tunda Joda, pastor of Christ's Chapel, International churches. I had met Dr. Chris Joda several years earlier at the New Life Christian Book store in Queens, New York. As I was walking down the aisle I saw an African gentleman reading a book. I noticed the book was The Biblical Principles of Success, my first book. The gentleman looked up. He saw the picture on the book, and he asked, "Is this you?"

I said, "Yes." So we got into a conversation and we noticed there were many different people in ministry that we were both familiar with. He invited me to come to his church, Christ's Chapel in London. I said I would be honored to come. About three months later I got a call from one of the ministers at Christ's Chapel in London, and indeed we did receive an invitation to minister in London.

At that time Brenda, Yolanda and I went to London and conducted a three-day revival. The results of the revival were tremendous. Many souls were saved and people were encouraged in the Word. Eventually, Dr. Joda invited me to come to the headquarters church in Lagos, Nigeria.

Now the church in Lagos is not just one church. There are 49 churches that Dr. Joda has in Nigeria, so it was a distinct honor and a privilege to be invited to conduct revival meetings in Lagos, Nigeria.

It was a very long flight. Before I even got onboard the plane, I noticed there were several people who were having problems with their luggage. If you had more than two bags they would charge you by the pound for bags. And there was one lady who had several bags so she had to pay $900. I said, "Lord, you know I've got this ticket, but I was not prepared to put out those additional funds."

So the Lord worked it out. When they weighed my bags, I did have additional pounds but they said, "Reverend, you just go on through." I thanked God because that was the first blessings of my trip.

Great Expectations

When I got on the plane and was seated, the plane took off. I couldn't go to sleep. There was an expectation of going to Africa, back to the mother land where civilization began, to the place where creation took place. I saw where Adam and Eve once were, where everything began--the motherland, Africa.

So I just stayed up, read my Bible, looked over some notes and prayed. We were in the air for well over 10 hours. There was a stop in Ghana for about three hours. After that we went to Lagos, Nigeria.

When I got off the plane, I wanted to kiss the ground, I felt like I was at home. As I looked out I saw nothing but a sea of black faces. The only other experience I had like that was the first time I went to Harlem. When I looked around I saw nothing but a sea of black faces. For an African-American man, that is an exhilarating feeling. It is a great experience to be a part of your roots and heritage. It's an experience that is incomparable to anything else. The only thing that would be higher than that would be, of course, giving one's life to Christ or maybe going on a trip to Jerusalem and walking where Jesus walked. This was a tremendous experience.

So, once I got off the plane, in the airport in Nigeria, there were representatives from Christ's Chapel, International Churches that met me. They knew who I was immediately. There was a line of about 300 people, and they quickly got me through customs. One of the deaconesses of the church worked at the airport so she just took my passport, visa and information, and in a matter of seconds we passed through customs and were in the car heading to the Christ's Chapel headquarters.

In the Midst of Great People

Once we arrived at the Christ's Chapel headquarters, I saw my good friend and mentor in the ministry, Dr. Chris Tunda Joda. We embraced. The last time I saw Dr. Joda was in New York. Now here we were in the mother land. Dr. Joda is a very special person, educated in some of the finest universities of the world. He is a licensed medical doctor and could have had a very lucrative practice, but he gave it up to help his brothers and sisters in Nigeria, and give them medical care for free. Also, he went into the ministry and became a pastor.

When Dr. Joda became a pastor in Nigeria, there was a lot of tradition. Many of the churches were into traditionalism. There were several main line churches and denominational churches, but neither stressed the importance of the baptism of the Holy Spirit or divine healing. When Dr. Joda began to pastor, it had a major impact upon Nigeria. Many of the churches had to dust off their Bibles and really dive back into the scriptures. Dr. Joda started Christ's Chapel with one mother church, but it eventually grew into 49 churches. It's still growing. I'm pretty sure when we were there for the revival, the 50th church was birthed somewhere. And they'll go on to 51 and beyond. I'm pretty sure by the time we return it will be 100 churches.

Keep the Fire Burning

This is a man who has a heart for people. He has a burden for revival, a burden for lost souls, a burden for Africa. We are in no way suggesting that the people of Africa are crying out, "Help! We need revival." asking the great Americans to come and to be the pioneers of revival in Africa.

What I found is that they were already experiencing revival in Africa. My job was to come in and encourage them to keep the fire burning. And if there was an area that had not experienced this revival, a revival which has brought about the birth of 49 additional churches, well then my responsibilities were to go into those areas and encourage them to experience revival fire.

When I went into the headquarters of Christ's Chapel and embraced my good friend, Dr. Joda, immediately he said, "Are you ready to preach?'

Now mind you, I had just gotten off the plane, so I said, "Yes, I'm ready." Two hours later I was there at the mother church in Lagos, Nigeria preaching. Of course prior to this, I had two hours to freshen up and get myself together. I met my roommate and we stayed at headquarters, Christ's Chapel. At the headquarters they had, in the basement, a place where they duplicated all of the tapes. They had a department where the young men and young women would make signs. You would see the signs and the posters of the meetings posted throughout Nigeria. Every place that you went, you saw the signs for this revival meeting.

Take It Back

The theme of the revival meeting was "The Violent Take It By Force." The kingdom of heaven suffereth violence, and the violent take it by force. Of course we know that Jesus said, "Turn the other cheek." We also know that when it came time for Jesus to go into the temple, and He saw the money changers

161

there, He picked up a rod and beat them. He got violent in the
positive sense, and let them know that "My Father's house is a
house of worship, and not a den of thieves." If you call
somebody a name, or you slap them or something, that's not
going to hurt who they are, nor is it any type of threat.

But when you mess with somebody's family, you know as
Jesus said, "My Father's house is a house of worship." Then you
know those are fighting terms. And the theme of this revival
really showed that the violent have to take it by force. There is a
time when Christians must stand up to take back what the devil
has stolen. Take back our family, take back our community, take
back our sons, and our daughters.

Dr. Joda, is doing a tremendous work in Lagos, Nigeria.

As I was saying earlier, everybody had work to do. I mean, I
met at least 50 people by the time I walked in the building.
Before I went upstairs I met different pastors. Outside there were
young men who were escorting speakers and preachers to the
various conferences.

Organizing God's Work

Then when I went to the second floor, they had a place
where they made the video tapes. And then a section where they
took care of business, mailing letters and things that had to go
out. And then they had a section where they would feed the
speakers, singers and the dancers. On the other side they had
bedrooms where the speakers retired for the night.

My roommate was Rev. John Taylor from London, England.
Brother Taylor and I ministered together that night. He was a
powerful preacher. The anointing of the Holy Spirit came upon
him in an awesome way. He could seldom get through a sermon
the majority of the time. The Holy Spirit would begin to use him
through a word of knowledge and then people received divine
touches from God and miraculous healings.

Spiritual Destiny

The night that I preached I shared the message, "Walking Through the Doorways of Destiny." There was a tremendous sense of destiny, a tremendous sense of God's purpose and God's plan for our lives. I have never felt such a connection with my destiny as I did that night in the mother land. I'm referring to that divine, preordained plan of God's will that says that God never ever changes His mind.

I ministered that night and the anointing of the Holy Spirit was tangible. You could feel the power of God in the atmosphere. There was a very strong spirit of praise and worship in the building.

After I finished ministering, Brother Whyte assisted me and escorted me out of the building. There were some gentlemen in the car, and they took me back to the ministry headquarters. Brother Whyte, Brother Jack June, Brother Isaac and Brother Dale stayed with me and assisted me in ministry while I was in Lagos, Nigeria. I will never forget them. Brother Whyte, Brother Jack June, Isaac and Dale--I can see their faces as I mention their names. They were servants of God in the most positive sense of the word. Anything that we needed, they were there to help.

A Strong Move of the Holy Spirit

I was touched by the respect, the compassion, and the love these friends had for the things of God, and for the people of God. As Brother Whyte escorted me out of the building, the praises of God were going forth fervently even as I walked outside the building. People were worshipping, praising God, and weeping. This touched me so deeply. When I got into the car, I had the driver to pray, the person in the passenger seat to pray, Brother Whyte to pray, and then I prayed. And we made that our custom while we were in Africa. Before I went into the meeting, and after we came out of the meeting, we all prayed. Also Rev. John Taylor from London, England was there and he also prayed in the car. We would start the meeting off with prayer, and we would seal it in prayer. And even when we got back to the ministry headquarters, Rev. John Taylor and myself that night stayed up and prayed for a good while.

Then we talked about what God was doing, in the sense of expectation, in terms of the manifestation of God's Spirit. We desired to know that we were in revival, that this wasn't something we were merely talking about, but this is something that we were actually living in, seeing with our own eyes a work of God who was doing His work in the midst of the years.

The following morning we got up around six. At seven o'clock Brother Whyte and Brother June Jack knocked on the door. They gave us notes saying that Rev. John Taylor would be going to the church outside of Lagos. They gave me a note saying that I would be going to Abeukuta, an African village about an hour and 30 minutes outside of Lagos.

A Multiple Impact

So we prepared. Early that morning June Jack and Brother Whyte returned. June Jack and Rev. John Taylor got into the van. And then Brother Whyte escorted me down-stairs. I went with Brother Isaac and Dale. We got into one of Christ's Chapel vans. Dr. Joda encouraged our hearts and told us just to go to the various villages and share the Word. He explained that the main service was going on at the National Nigerian stadium, but simultaneously, there were services going on in all 49 churches. This was to create a multiple impact.

So we were just excited about this, because this really drove home a message: "The violent take it by force," taking back what the devil has stolen. It was not just giving the devil one punch, but it was a devastating blow. When you have one service going on, if you have the service where you had hundreds of thousands giving their lives to the Lord, in 49 other churches you had the same thing going on. It was a multiple impact, and it devastated Satan's kingdom in Africa.

164

There was an overflow of people and there were crowds standing in the streets who wanted to come into the stadium. However, they couldn't get in, so they just stayed out and prayed and gave their lives to the Lord right on the street outside the stadium.

Then we went on to Abeukuta. Brother Isaac and Dale, and a pastor in Abeukuta, Pastor Beadorf were in our party. Pastor Beadorf was a great man of God, a young man who had compassion for the people. As we were approaching the village of Abeukuta, we were stopped by security guards at the various check points who looked in and examined our vehicle. Isaac and Dale explained to them that we were from Christ's Chapel. Then they looked back to see me, and I was dressed in a dark suit, and a purple clergy shirt. I had no problems with the security or the police during my visit. There were other speakers who had some problems with the police but I felt so at home in Africa. It was just like, "Hey, brother, God bless you."

Where Jesus Sends Me I'll Go

As we were entering Abeukuta I saw different African huts. There were men and women washing up outside. Some of them were dressed in cloths covering up themselves but wearing nothing elaborate. But as we got closer to Abeukuta, we began to see some beautiful homes. The hotel we stayed in was a wonderful facility.

That Sunday we went to the church where the meeting was to take place. It was made of a slab of stone for the walls. A door space was cut out but there was no door. It was an open-air church. So the people came to the meeting, some of them lived in homes and some of them may have come from huts.

The first service was held that night. The worship and praise that went forth was tremendous. They had electric guitars, and drums and they would just begin praising God. You could sense the presence of the Holy Spirit in the atmosphere.

We came into the service. I sat down, and within five minutes Pastor Beaurdorf introduced me. I led the people in a chorus of, "Give thanks with a grateful heart." I was extremely thankful to God for this opportunity to come to the motherland. After the song I went into the message.

The Presence of the Holy Spirit

The Holy Spirit began to move in that place, it was a modern day Pentecost there. Many people received deliverance and hope to bring about change in their community. They realized that their lives could make a difference in their community. Also, a strong prophetic word went forth that night to encourage the people gathered.

We stayed there and did two other services. I will never forget Abeukuta and the people. I will never forget the tremendous outpouring of the Holy Spirit and the revival flames that burned for the things of God. In both Abeukuta and Nigeria the people were very poor, but they were rich in God's mercy. The majority of the people were hard working people with dignity, people with respect. Before I left for Abeukuta Pastor Beaudorf presented me with an African outfit--a beautiful orange, blue and white African outfit. For me, that was the greatest honor. I had an authentic African outfit from the motherland made from material that comes from the motherland. That touched my heart and touched my soul.

Led of the Lord

After we did the last service there in Abeukuta, Pastor Beaudorf wanted us to stay for another service, but we had to get back to Nigeria. And after I returned from Abeukuta, the Holy Spirit laid it on my heart to fast. I'm glad I followed the leading of the Holy Spirit. Sure enough, when I called home to New York, I found out that there was a young man in the church who had gotten into some trouble with the law. We kept him in prayer and stood on God's Word with fasting and prayer.

During this time, I preached at the National Nigerian stadium. The experience of going into the stadium to preach the gospel to people who came from all parts of Africa was a special blessing. Also there were people who came from London, people who came from Atlanta, Georgia and from as far away as Liverpool and South Africa. It was one of the highlights of my ministry, to share the gospel of Jesus Christ in the place where civilization began. Also, I realize that Satan was very angry because the oppression that you see in Africa is really due to the fact that he knows that this is where it all began. Most scientists, archaeologists and people in these fields, have come to the point of realizing that this is a truthful statement. But the greater message of importance is that we were taking back what the devil has stolen.

Revival Ensures Hope

So when I shared messages like the Biblical Principles of Success, I'm sure this was a life and death message for them. Getting God's Biblical Principles of Success meant walking in the wisdom of God, in the affairs of life, and that meant everything. It meant their spiritual fellowship with God; it meant relationships between husband and wife, mother and father, son and daughter. It gave the motivation that they needed to excel in life, even in the midst of hopeless situations. It was a life-or-death message for them.

And there was a hunger for the Word of God. People would come out early in the morning. Services began at nine o'clock but sometimes worshipers arrived at seven. They would wait outside until the doors of the stadium opened and they would stay from nine in the morning to 11 o'clock at night, even if it meant passing up breakfast, lunch and dinner. They wanted to hear the Word of God. There was such a tremendous appreciation for God's Word. There were times when someone would be preaching and the lights would go out, yet the preaching would still continue. The people would stay there, and

167

when the lights came back on, everybody just praised God. It was this type of commitment to revival, this hunger, and this passion for God's Word. When we say, "Help! We need revival," really we're saying that in Africa they were experiencing revival.

World Wide Revival

We're to experience this world wide revival. As Joel wrote, "In the last days I will pour out My Spirit upon all flesh; your sons and daughters will prophesy, and that your old men will dream dreams, and your young men will see visions." That's the promise of world-wide revival. We have to look at what's going on in Nigeria. Look at what God is doing in that situation, through Christ's Chapel, and all over the world. As I talk about revival, every minister that I talk to tells me about a different city in the world that's experiencing revival. In foreword of, *Walking Through the Doorways of Destiny* [1] Pastor Donnie McClurkin writes: "Yet now, in these latter days, the church is experiencing a great awakening through the Holy Spirit. The body of Christ must be prepared with zeal and passion - for every spiritual encounter. We can meet the needs of our searching generation by increasing in knowledge, understanding, information and practical application of the principles essential for spiritual success."

It's going to take all of these things to encourage us to really get to the point where that world wide revival begins to happen. It takes a light shining in Africa. It takes a light shining in London. It takes a light shining in New York. It takes a light shining in Wyoming. It takes a light shining in all different parts of every country in the world. This light must shine until it gets to a point where the things that God has prophesied will come to pass. This is not something we do ourselves, but this should be prompted by the Holy Spirit.

A Burden for Lost Souls

After the first service at the National Nigerian stadium I came back the following day around three o'clock in the afternoon. I did another revival meeting and talked about the burden for revival. And if there was ever a place that I noticed the burden for revival, it was definitely in Nigeria. When Dr. Chris Joda gave an altar call, he would just wait. At first just a few people came. But he would wait. Then more would come. It was a great harvest of souls.

I was really impressed that well over 50 percent of the people who came to these revival meetings were men. These men came not just at one point of the meeting but early in the morning till late at night. From nine in the morning until eleven at night. Some of them did not have breakfast, lunch or dinner.

The burden they had for revival was tremendous. It was an inner yearning to bring about change in people's lives. When I saw all those men I thought about a passage entitled *One-Man Revival*, written by B. Carlisle and R. Thomas: [2]

"I need a one man revival. A renewing of my heart. To capture me before I stray too far."

A burden for revival was evident everywhere I went. Before I left to go to Nigeria, I ran into a young African man in the mall in New York. This was about two days before I was leaving to go to Nigeria. He told me that he was born and raised in Nigeria.

A Godly Reputation

I said, "I'm getting ready to go there to conduct a revival."

He said, "Well when you go, go to Christ's Chapel because they're experiencing revival in Lagos, Nigeria."

That shows how the move of God is very important. It is important because there might be some student who goes away to college in another area; if they receive a touch from God in the local church, they're going to encourage somebody else. "Hey, when you go to that area, stop by that church, because God is there."

169

See? That's what we need when we talk about revival. We need God to visit us. The scripture talks about not missing the time of our visitation. Many times we miss the time of our visitation, and there is divine visitation right now in Lagos, Nigeria.

A Divine Visitation

But beyond that, God wants to bring a divine visitation of the Holy Spirit across this whole world. God's bottom line is that He wants the knowledge of the glory of God to cover the earth as the waters cover the sea. The book of Habakkuk makes this point clear. The only way that this is going to happen is by having a world wide revival. Now when we talk about world-wide revival, we've got to realize that Satan is going to have his world wide revival while God is going to have His. Satan will bring that which is counterfeit, but God brings that which is authentic. We just have to stick to the authority of God's Word. If we do that, we'll be all right.

But getting back to this revival in Africa: In the second meeting at the National Nigerian Stadium I ministered the Word concerning the burden for revival. My text came from the book of Habakkuk and we'll discuss that later in more detail.

Another Side of Ministry

But in one of the night meetings I shared with my audience again about walking through the doorways of destiny. I shared with them some of the challenges that I faced coming to Lagos, I had problems getting things together in order to be able to come. But God worked out a lot of things in terms of resources. I had to work some extra hours and I did odd jobs that I would not do under normal circumstances. I even took a day where I worked in an animal shelter. I worked with dogs and I had fun doing it. I wanted to show another side of ministry, a side that shows I will do what is needed in order to get to where God wants us to go. I was there handing out forms, telling the people to fill out the forms, so their dogs can get a rabies shot. And this helped me to get the additional funds that I needed to be able to go to Nigeria.

No Struggle, No Progress

When we talk about destiny, you know, we see these big lights of destiny, fulfilling God's will and His purpose and that type of thing. But a lot of times we won't tell about the hard times. I feel that it's important to share about the hard times. There are people out there who are hurting. Then they see God begin to bless somebody, and they never hear about the difficulties and the challenges that they go through. They consider themselves some type of odd ball, because they're going through hell and high water. It doesn't seem like this person is going through anything.

When you read somebody's press release, or you see something about them on television or in the newspaper you know they went through something in order to be consider as a newsworthy subject. I'm a firm believer in the saying, "Without struggle there is no progress." A lot of times we don't want to talk about struggle, or we talk about struggle only in the negative sense. But for every negative there is a positive.

And so for everything that a minister could give up and talk about in the negative sense, there is something in the positive sense about that same issue. So God began to deal with me. It wasn't easy getting to Nigeria. And it wasn't easy getting back, but God did bless.

The last service that we conducted was in Ojokoro. The Pastor's name was Pastor Dota. This godly man had invited me to his office. He told me before I went out to preach that his wife died in a fire at the church the year before. My heart went out to this man in sympathy and prayer.

After she died in the fire, he was devastated. But through brokenness he sought the face of God. In the midst of his pain, the bitterness and the anguish, he received inner healing through

171

peace that passes all understanding. He still deals with the hurt, but you know, he's hooked into a power source through the Holy Spirit.

Inner Healing

People of the community were touched by that man. He didn't backslide. He didn't get hooked up with witch doctors and things like that. He sought the face of God, and he was a leader to his people. The people saw his compassion and his love for God, and the love he had for the people in Ojokoro. As a result, the church literally tripled in size. I mean, they really need to build a new building now.

We went there to conduct the last service. The message was, "Stir Up the Gift Within You." This was a timely message because there's an aspect of revival where God stirs things up. God stirs things up and God sets everything in motion. That's what we are really looking for in revival. Likely, there is also a response to that. Once God has stirred up things, He tells us, like the Apostle Paul tells Timothy, "Stir up the gift within you." You have experienced revival. Now since you have experienced revival, you have to go on into evangelism.

Stir Up the Gift

So in revival, God stirs things up. Then, after we have experienced that stirring God tells us, "My Spirit is in you, and I want you to stir up the gift that's within you, because a man's gift will make room for him, and bring him before great men."

The Thrust of Evangelism

That phrase "stir up the gift," means to fan the flame. We have to fan the flames of revival through evangelism. Revivals don't last forever, you know. Revivals are temporary, but evangelism is continuous. So if we see the connection between revival and evangelism, we can have more of the continuous flow of revival. We realize that revivals don't last forever. For example, the Azusa Street revival lasted for a period of time then faded. Look at the Welsh revival that also lasted for a period of time then faded. Charles Haddon Spurgeon states it best when he discussed *A Real and Lasting Revival*:

"I am glad of any signs of life, even if they should be feverish and transient, and I am slow to judge any well intended movement, but I am very fearful that many so called revivals in the long run wrought more harm than good. A species of religious gambling has fascinated many men, and given them a distaste for the sober business of true godliness. But if I would nail down counterfeits upon the counter, I do not therefore undervalue true gold. Far from it. It is to be desired beyond measure that the Lord would send a real and lasting revival of spiritual life."[3]

Share the Blessing

We have to learn that in order to experience world wide revival we must share. For example, I have shared the revival in Lagos, Nigeria. Somebody shares about revival in some other part of the world and encourages the church about what God has stirred up. Then comes a period of evangelism when we stir up the gift that's within us, the gift that God has put on us by the laying on of His hands.

As we begin to do that, the Holy Spirit will bring us from a revival into a flow of evangelism and then from a flow of evangelism back into revival. We can get a cycle going. After great revival you get a time of backsliding. That's what happens in many cases. People experience great revival, and people get saved. Then people get back into their old ways to the bickering, to the gossip, and just being church folk instead of being a good church. Andrew Murray writes, "A true revival means nothing less than a revolution, casting out the spirit of worldliness, making God's love triumph in the heart."[4]

Be Watchful

You lose many people as a result of backsliding into their old wicked ways. But if we develop the habit of going from revival into the work of evangelism, and back into the next revival we will see a change. Then we can get a connection there. We can fulfill what God has said is going to happen. It's a matter of destiny, it's going to happen, the only question is, Are we going to be a part of it?

Mordecai tells Esther that deliverance will come to the Jews, but will it come through you? Are you going to stand up? Are you going to move to the next level? Of course she finally comes to the point and says, "Well if I perish I perish, but I'm going to see the king." I'm moving to the next level. "I'm not just going to be a little barbie doll, just a pretty face. I'm going to stand up for what I believe in, even if it puts my life on the line."

That's what it takes for real revival to come forth. And when I say "revival", I'm not talking just about the service. I'm talking about something that brings changes--changes that bring about political, social, and economic changes as well.

A Spirit of Compassion

Our last African meeting was held in Ojokoro. Pastor Dato had lost his wife, but here we were in his church. The membership had tripled in size and I was ministering to these people. I felt tremendous compassion toward them. I felt the same compassion during the third night of the revival meeting at the National Nigerian Stadium where I had a healing service. Hundreds of people came that night for healing. The lines just continued on and on.

For example, you'd have a line of 50 people. After I prayed for them another line would come forth and it just went on continuously. I felt the compassion of Jesus, especially when I prayed for two little babies. I don't remember the exact sickness they had, but I dropped to my knees as I prayed for them. I felt the compassion of Jesus come upon me when I prayed for the people in Ojokoro. It was my last meeting there in Africa.

After that meeting was over, I went back to the ministry headquarters to see Dr. Joda and my good friend, Pastor Michael Burns, who also went on the trip. We preached in several of the African villages as well as in the National Nigerian stadium. It was a distinct honor for Mike to come. I've known him since he was a teenager. I joined up with Mike when he had just graduated from Bible school. We'd preach on the streets of Roosevelt, and we'd witness as we held meetings together. It was an honor to work with him. Who would have thought that 16 years later we would be going forth, doing the work of the Lord together. God enabled us to minister in another country and take our Christian service to another level.

A Great Experience

As we prepared to leave I thanked God again and again for the opportunity to witness revival and such an outpour of His spirit--not just to preach about it, but to experience it, and that's very important. We should all say, "Lord, I just don't want to *talk* about these things, and *read* about these things. I want to *experience Pentecost.* I want to walk in the things that the Bible talks about and for them to be a reality."

When it was time to leave, Dr. Joda's people took us to the airport. Pastor Mike was also going to the airport. He was planning to go to a meeting in another African city. But that did not work out. They wanted to charge him an astronomical price for his bags. It would have been almost twice the amount of his ticket coming and going. So he ended up staying another week, continuing on with the revival meeting. This wasn't just a week of services; it was revival--a revival that birthed several others into an organization that boasts phenomenal growth. So this is a continuous revival, because it's still going on to this very day.

Bishop T.D. Jakes declares: "I believe that we're in the beginning stages of the greatest revival this world has ever known. In order for us to carry out the plan of God, we must realize that divine intervention and not human effort will usher in this end-time revival. Christians must know that their lives with God can be full of new experiences every day. Instead of merely enduring our salvation, we can enjoy the fullness that God has provided in Holy Ghost."[5]

On the Way Home

The people from Christ Chapel worked everything out for my flight home. However, on our way to the airport, one of the vans got stuck in a pot hole. The men from the ministry dug out the van.

When I got on the plane, we flew first to Ghana where I arrived about one o'clock in the morning. I was supposed to catch a connecting flight that would take me to JFK in New York. But the connecting flight in Ghana was delayed. I later learned from a reliable source that there was a strong possibility that the plane was taken to Lybia to meet with Khadafi.

Needless to say, the plane was not available, so I said, "Well, if the plane was taken to Libya or wherever, I'm just glad that I wasn't on it. Thank God they waited till we got off."

But the airline was very helpful to us, they put us up in a hotel that night, then gave us breakfast the following morning. We caught a plane early that morning to JFK, but when my family came to pick me up, you know, they were quite disturbed. My wife, Brenda, at this time was six months pregnant with our son Jordan so she was just resting up. My parents came to pick me up. They were there to pick me up, but originally my flight was supposed to arrive at seven in the morning, but when they got there they saw "delayed."

A Few Delays But It Was Worth It

They asked airport personnel and the people didn't know what happened. Well the plane was taken by the military, supposedly, but they didn't know exactly what happened. So they asked, and they asked, and no one could give them an explanation. I arrived in New York around five-thirty in the afternoon. I should have arrived at seven in the morning. We were in the air, and we had to stop in another African city because when the military took the plane they did not refuel, so we had to stop and refuel. That added several hours more to the trip.

During all of this, I took time to reflect and thank God that He gave me the privilege to go to the motherland where it all began, in terms of His creation. And it was the greatest ministerial experience I have ever had. It's something that I don't take for granted. It gave me a whole new understanding, and a fresh new outlook on what revival really is and how a move of God can change the lives of ordinary people.

A Time To Reflect

During the delays, I thought about all the young men I've seen in prison.

I thought about how Dr. Joda was impacting lives through the power of God, impacting the lives of literally thousands of young men, and how these young men have become part of his ministry. And he's got them all working. Some of them are making posters, some are reproducing tapes and some are working with the ministry. But everyone had something to do. It gave them a sense of purpose and dignity. It just moved me to see so many young men active in ministry. Not active in ministry as a preacher or a pastor, or teacher or prophet, although there are plenty of worshipers who serve in this capacity. Nevertheless, they were active in the ministry of helps, in positions that you would normally see women in. Of course we

177

need men and of course we need women, but in the United States we don't see these large numbers of men going forth.

Women would love to have it. That really touched my heart. Also to see that the men were not sexist. They were open to women being used of God. There were women who were touched in this revival, God used them tremendously and Dr. Joda was open to that. Of course, I encourage women to work in the ministry regardless of national origin. God is an equal opportunity employer and God is not sexist. He said that in the last days, "I will pour out of My Spirit upon all flesh." Notice that *all flesh.* "That your sons and daughters will prophesy." God is not sexist. God is always an equal opportunity employer.

After Revival Comes Satanic Retaliation

I want to share what happened after I got back from Africa. You know, it's great to talk about this great revival in Africa, but I experienced some of the greatest satanic attacks after I returned from Africa. This experience is very important for young evangelists, preachers, teachers, prophets and saints of God to read about. Arthur L. Mackey, Jr. went through some hard times, but I count it all as gain for the cause of Christ.

I'm standing on God's Word. I'm praying, confessing my faults, and I have never in my entire life felt closer to the Lord. I never felt more connected with my God-given destiny. This is a time when I'm spiritually connected.

No other time have I experienced such a satanic attack. After this blessed trip to Africa, everything possible went wrong. Satan was angry because we hit him with a multiple impact. Every great thing that happened at the revival in Africa happened simultaneously at 49 other churches.

So we put a bruising on our enemy. And of course he wants to retaliate. But the Word says, "Having done all to stand. Stand, therefore..." You've got to put on the helmet of salvation. You've got to put on the breastplate of righteousness. You have to wield the sword of the Spirit, we have to have our feet shod with the preparation of the gospel of peace, and having done all to stand. We've got to stand therefore in the midst of the hell, and in the midst of the high water.

Remain Focused in the Time of Trouble

When I got back, my wife and I had problems with both cars. I literally had to shell out thousands of dollars--money needed to be used for other bills. Now I don't have to share this, but I'm sharing this to let people know that they are not crazy when they're going through hard times. Of course, this is light compared to some of the things Satan tries to come against us with. But sometimes you go through hard times, and you go through major struggles simply because you are serving God because you are experiencing revival. Anything that Satan can find to come against you, he will use.

Then there are some things that you just have no explanation for. You've just got to learn how to give God the praise and glory. As I've explained in my book "Walking Through The Doorways Of Destiny," you may experience great hardships, but some of the greatest doorways have been divinely opened. God calls it, "a door that no man can close." But, of course, with every door that God opens, there are adversaries that come against us. But we've got to keep our focus on Jesus. I want to encourage people, in terms of revival: keep your eyes focused on the Lord.

"I press towards the mark of the high calling in Christ Jesus." Not in myself. You could have an experience where you call fire down from heaven and you may conduct a great revival where false prophets are slain. But, the next day you'll be running from a Jezebel.

A Still Voice

God doesn't want us to get into the show of His power, but He wants His power to be in our hearts.

And remember the story of Elijah. He's hiding, he waits to hear God and thunder, and then the storm, and then fire, and he doesn't hear God through any of that, but he hears God in the still, small voice. And if you want to have the fire of revival, and all these types of things, you've really got to focus on hearing that small still voice.

If you don't hear that small, still voice, that speaks to your heart, then you're really not going to make it to heaven. What's really going to make the difference is that we know Him. Most certainly there will be people who will say, "Jesus, I preached in your Name Lord, I cast out demons in your Name, I healed the sick in your Name." But He's going to say, "Depart from Me, you workers of iniquity."

Workers of iniquity? They said that they healed the sick, they cast out demons, and they were doing great work for the Lord. No, but they never knew Him. It is not enough to know about revival. You must know the Lord of revival. It's not enough to know about the work of God, you must be in a right relationship with the Lord who has called you to that work. We've got to know the Lord of revival personally for ourselves, in an intimate way.

Excellent Hospitality

When I was in Africa, I saw many brothers and sisters who knew the Lord in an intimate manner. For example, when you talked to them you could feel the love of God, and when they prepared the food, it was a ministry. Oh, some of the best food I've ever tasted was food that I ate while in Africa. Oh my God, I had some sugar cane, I loved it. The rice and the chicken--it was mouth watering delicious. I love the way they prepared the food, and the way that they put it together. The hospitality was second to none, I've never gone to a country where the people were so hospitable. You know, it was just tremendous, a highlight of my life, going to Africa, and experiencing the hospitality of the people. Nowhere in America can I compare the hospitality. I went to school in the south, and I know about the southern hospitality and it's great. But it could not compare to the hospitality of the folk there in Africa.

But greater than hospitality are the people in Africa. They were really in touch with the move of God. What God was doing to bring it on home, in terms of the things He wants to do in our life, in terms of bringing that spiritual move, bringing the revival, bringing inner healing, bringing a central fullness, bringing us back to where He wants us to be.

The Need for Revival

So these things we have to ponder and crave when we think about the need for revival. It's happening in Lagos, Nigeria but is it happening in your home church? Is it happening in your community? Is it happening in your city? Well God can use you to be an agent of revival. God can use you to be an agent of spiritual renewal.

Just as He used Dr. Chris Tunde Joda. Now there is Christ's Chapel with 49 sister churches in Lagos, Nigeria. He has a church in London, one in Canada, some in the United States, but all of this constitutes revival. This is the Lord renewing His work in the midst of the years. All right, this is nothing new to God, this has been in the mind of God. This is a matter of destiny but now it's being fulfilled in this world. A revival, God brings to life that which was always there, but was just dead and dormant.

There are some things that are again, and there are some things that are dormant in you. God is calling them to be resurrected, as He called Lazarus from the grave. There's a Lazarus within your life. There's a Lazarus in your life that God is calling. No matter what that is. It could be a dead marriage. It could be a dead ministry. Could be a dead relationship with a father and a daughter, a mother and a son. Whatever it is, God is calling it to rise up from the dead. He calls us to come forth.

181

Arthur L. Mackey, Jr.

An Agent for Revival

Somebody who may have been denying that they were called into the ministry, but they know that God has called. God is calling you just to go and pray with the people in hospitals, the cancer patients, or the AIDS's patient. God is calling you to rise up in Him. He's calling you to be an agent of revival.

We're trying to make that word much bigger than what it really means. Revival is just bringing back to life that which was dead. If we really admit it, there are a lot of situations in our lives, and we need to be resurrected. Only God can do that. When we realize that only God can do it, and we humble ourselves under His mighty hand, then He'll exalt us in due time. It's not by our might, it's not by our power, it's not by our ability, but it's by His Spirit, saith the Lord.

PART FOUR:

THE REVIVAL LIFESTYLE

Chapter 10

THE QUEST FOR SPIRITUAL RENEWAL - TAKING IT ONE DAY AT A TIME

The Word of God

The entire fourth chapter of Second Corinthians is a word from the Lord:

"Therefore seeing we have this ministry, as we have received mercy, we faint not; but have renounced the hidden things of dishonesty, not walking in craftiness, nor handling the Word of God deceitfully; but by the manifestation of the truth commending ourselves to every man's conscience in the sight of God.

"But if our gospel be hid, it is hid to them that are lost; in whom the god of this world has blinded the minds of them which believe not, lest the light of the glorious gospel of Christ, who is the image of God, should shine upon them. For we preach not ourselves, but Christ Jesus the Lord; and ourselves your servants for Jesus' sake. For God, who commanded the light to shine out of darkness, hath shined in our hearts, to give the light of the knowledge of the glory of God in the face of Jesus Christ.

"But we have this treasure in earthen vessels, that the excellency of the power may be of God, and not of us. We are troubled on every side; yet not distressed; we are perplexed, but not in despair; persecuted, but not forsaken; cast down, but not destroyed; always bearing about in the body the dying of the Lord Jesus, that the life also of Jesus might be made manifest in our body.

"For we which live are always delivered unto death for Jesus' sake, that the life also of Jesus might be made manifest in our mortal flesh. So then death worketh in us, but life in you. We having the same spirit of faith, according as it is written, I believed, and therefore I have spoken; we also believe, and therefore speak; knowing that He which raised up the Lord Jesus shall raise up us also by Jesus, and shall present us with you.

"For all things are for your sakes, that the abundant grace might through the thanksgiving of many redound to the glory of God. For which cause we faint not; but though our outward man perish, yet the inward man is renewed day by day. For our light affliction, which is but for a moment, worketh for us a far more exceeding and eternal weight of glory; while we look not at the things which are seen, but at the things which are not seen; for the things which are seen are temporal; but the things which are not seen are eternal."

And we want to focus on that 16th verse, it says, "For which cause we faint not; but though our outward man perish, yet the inward man is renewed day by day." And we like to talk about "The Quest For Spiritual Renewal."

A Spiritual Mission

My brothers and sister, I am on a journey. I have embarked upon a pursuit, a mission, a search, and a quest for spiritual renewal. I've come to the realization that I don't know everything that there is to know about God. The more I meditate upon the scriptures, the more I ponder various passages in God's Word, the more I discover that I need to learn more of Him. I yearn to draw closer to His heart, to His will and to His ways.

In essence, that is what spiritual renewal and revival is all about. Many times we begin to grow stale in our religion and in our relationship with God. We come to church, we go to the various programs, we go to the various functions. There is a form of Godliness, but it denies the power thereof. We need the power and the fire of the Holy Ghost. And not just for Sunday morning worship. It's easy to worship, to praise God and to shout when all the brothers and sisters are here. That is important, because the Bible tells us not to forsake the assembling of the brethren. That is a support system and there is encouragement that we receive from one another. Just when you walk through the door, your mere presence is important. Every life is a testimony. Everybody has something that they're going through. It's just the fact that you came out to church, with all the hell fire that you're going through, that's a testimony.

Renewal of the Spirit

But when we begin to move into spiritual renewal, not only is this service a priority, but the things that we talk about in worship become a lifestyle for us. They begin to impact us more when we're out on the corner talking to the widow's boy… when the women are in the hair salon, or when the men are in the barber shop. It begins to roll over into every aspect of our life. There is a yearning to come closer to Him. There is this quest, journey, or march towards revival in our lives. Revival personally, but also revival corporately. Revival in our homes, but also revival in our churches; revival in our prayer closets, but also revival in our public schools, and revival in our communities.

The Bible says, "Faith cometh by hearing, and hearing by the Word of God." So it's the subjects that we talk about. This is not a push-it-under-the-rug ministry. It's not the, ignore-the-situation ministry, but the things that we deal with, God gives us an "in time" word to deal with problems.

If we talk about praise and worship, our faith begins to get built up in the area of praise and worship, and that's an area in which we become strong. But if we don't talk about finances, we can be strong in praise and worship, and weak in finances. Or, we can preach about salvation, but if we don't preach about God's healing power, then we would be strong in one area, and weak in another area. "Faith cometh by hearing, and hearing by the Word of God."

We Have a Ministry

So we want to build up our faith in the area of spiritual renewal. We must be on a quest. We must be on a journey. This must be a concrete decision that we make, because God has already made His decision. He says, "I chose you, you didn't choose Me." Any decisions that we make, it's because He chose us first of all. God made a decision that you would be here at church this morning, because He knew exactly what you needed. He has it right here for you. You don't have to go anyplace else. He has the answer to your problems, He is your solution.

In the 4th chapter of 2nd Corinthians Paul begins by saying, "For we have this ministry." That is our challenge, that is our blessing. But that is our dilemma, too. That is my first point, this ministry that the Lord has given us. And ministry 101 teaches us that everybody has a ministry. Most times we think that only those who are called to the five-fold ministry are the ones who have a true ministry, that you must be an apostle, or teacher, or pastor, or prophet or evangelist.

Different Types of Ministries

But that represents the five different "preachers" that God has set in His church. Most of the time we talk about a preacher in the sense of whether he moans or he groans, or he teaches, or this, or that. But God doesn't break it down that way. God has five categories of preachers: the apostle, the teacher, the prophet, the evangelist and the pastor. All who are called into the ministry have one of those types of ministries, or they might have a combination or they might even have all five.

But it doesn't stop there. For everyone who is saved, everyone who confesses Jesus with his or her mouth, and believes that He was raised from the dead, has a ministry. But Jesus will come into our lives and save us. He did that 2000 years ago on Calvary. The only thing we do is receive it.

Godly Influence

Anyone can be saved. But once we give our lives to the Lord, and He saves our soul, we have a ministry. Not only that, we have a service. We have a work for the Lord. The young men and the young women of our congregation have a work for the Lord: it is to evangelize others within your realm of influence. Some people will not listen to everything that I say. The reply is, "Well, he's a preacher. He's grown up, and he's been in the church. Oh, how does he know about what I'm living, and what I'm going through?"

But God has also given you a ministry. There might be people you can relate to, or people you can reach. But I may never be able to reach them. There are those who work in the music ministry, a powerful calling. In the Bible, what tribe did they send out in war? They sent out Judah first. They sent out the ones whose name meant praise and worship. They sang unto the Lord. Why? Because God wants the praise. He wants the worship. Before anything happens, God wants to get the glory. Our God is a jealous God. It's not Buddha that's in control. It's not Mohammed, but we have to lift up the Name of Jesus.

Jesus said, "If I be lifted up, I will draw all men unto Me." Neil T. Anderson and Elmer L. Towns support this quote well: "This is an exciting time to be alive. Not since the Day of Pentecost have we seen such phenomenal growth of the Church world wide. Africa was less than 5 percent Christian at the turn of the century; it is expected to be 50 percent Christian by the end of this millennium. China had only about 5 million believers when communism took control of the country. Now the estimates vary from 50 to as high as 180 million believers. Missiologists estimate that between 25,000 and 35,000 are coming to Christ daily in China. Indonesia is the world's most populated Muslim nation, but the percentage of Christians has been progressing so rapidly that the government won't release accurate figures."[1]

So we have this ministry. God is giving us this responsibility. He doesn't want us to play with it. He doesn't want us to drop it.

Ministry Oriented

It says, "Therefore seeing we have this ministry, as we have received mercy...." Now sometimes we don't deserve to be a preacher, a trustee, a deacon, a member of the church, or a member of a choir but it's the mercy of God that allows these things. Because God is present, He's been with us all the time. He knows everything that we did right. He knows everything that we did wrong. So it's because of mercy that we're serving in ministry.

So God is calling us to change our thinking from being religious orientated to being more ministry orientated. This is a work of the Lord. This is a service that I am rendering unto Him. And it says, "Therefore we have received this ministry as we have received mercy, and we faint not." But there are many who are fainting, many who have given up on this journey.

Godly Motives

This journey has to be more than just any old walk. It's not a walk that we can just jump in and jump out of. This is something that we must be totally committed to. We must renounce the hidden things of dishonesty, and not hold the Word of God in deception. There must not be an ulterior motive, but there must be a God motive. A God motive is when people's lives can be changed. If they drink liquor or alcohol they can be delivered by the power of God.

The brother or sister who's shooting up drugs can be delivered by the power of God. God's healing power is alive and present today. We must preach this gospel, and not preach it deceitfully, but preach it uncompromisingly, because the Word says that "If our gospel be hid, it is hid to them that are lost." We have this ministry, this quest for spiritual renewal--not just

189

for pulpit ministry, but for our own spiritual ministry. We come to church, to be renewed and to be revived. So when we deal with our families, communities and co-workers, we desire that our ministry be activated by the Holy Spirit.

Under Contract

I'm talking about everything that we say, I'm talking about everything that we do, I'm talking about every step that we take. It's either going to be a ministry unto God or it's going to be a breach of contract.

When we got saved, we actually were making a contract with Jesus that we were going to live for him. So many times we just accept Him as Savior, but we've got to let Him be Lord of our life. We've got to let Him be in the driver's seat and take control. God says, "For we have this ministry," and we've got to do something. This isn't preaching about Rev. Arthur Mackey, Jr., or preaching about the deacons, trustees, or the congregation. It's preaching Jesus Christ.

That's where the deliverance is. That's where the power is. And when the devil comes up against it, he knows if we're coming in the Name of Jesus, because he knows Jesus. He knew the apostle Paul. I remember the seven sons of Scieva who tried to cast out demons, and the demons just ripped them to shreds. "Paul we know, Jesus we know, but we don't know who you are." "You're not associated with Jesus. You're not associated with the God of Paul."

So we've got to be real for the Lord, because when we come up against demons, it's no plain matter. When we come against situations where the devil is just trying to wreck lives, and bring havoc in people's homes, and in situations in their families, we've got to have the power of God upon us.

Heavenly Treasure

So not only do we have this ministry, but verse 7 says that secondly, "we have a treasure in earthen vessels." This ministry is a treasure in a physical body--a physical body that will eventually die, a physical body that's full of faults, a body in which we are created in the image of God. Yet we are not fully perfect like God. We strive towards perfection.

The Word says, "Be ye holy, because I am holy." It's something that we have to do because He has told us to do it. He knows what is best for us. He calls us into the process of sanctification, where we begin to live for Him, we begin to seek Him, to change our ways, to change our attitudes. God wants to deal with our attitudes. God wants to deal with our lying tongue, and God wants to deal with the thoughts within our minds. He wants to transform us, but in spite of all of these problems, He says that we do have this ministry, that we do have this treasure.

Activate Your Ministry

Sometimes we put it into a book and we get that book out there and that message, that is ministry. Going into foreign countries and preaching the gospel, that is ministry. Somebody is down and out on your job. Somebody died in their family, or they're going through a divorce, or there is a situation that has them totally depressed, and you go to them and share a word of prayer, that is ministry.

The Bible says, "Keep your heart with all diligence, for out of it come the issues of life." We've got to guard this ministry. We've got to guard this treasure. We've got to guard this gift that God has given to us. We just can't take it for granted that we have the message, because we have the message that can change the world. We've got to believe in that message. "Faith cometh by hearing, and hearing by the Word of God." You've got to believe in this quest for spiritual renewal. We've got to believe deep down in our heart that this is what will change our community.

191

The Lord Will Bring You Out

One thing I found that we have to do is begin to look at what God did in the past. When we begin to see how God has brought us out before, I'm sure that we can make it. Remember how He brought you out in the past, and remember to praise Him in the present. Remember what He brought you out of in the past--the mess, the muck and the mire. Remember to praise Him in your present problem and predicament. You will come out, you will come out of that situation, because God has delivered us before. And if He did it before, He can do it again.

And if there is not anything else that works, I know for sure that that works. Too many people are praising themselves, lifting themselves up. But it's Jesus who has to be lifted up. This body is ashes to ashes and dust to dust. God took us out of the dust of the earth, and blew into us the breath of life, and man became a living soul.

Your Life Is Your Ministry

If we get too arrogant, God can remind us, ashes to ashes, and dust to dust. We're all going to have to return to the dust, so we've got to be grateful for this time, this span of grace that He's given us. This little pinch of grace, to get a little reviving. This little space of grace that He's given to us, we have to do something with our life, because our life is our ministry.

If you weren't listening, that's what I'm getting at. Our life is our ministry. "My life is my ministry." "Your life is your ministry." "Our lives are God's ministry." We are the body of what? Of Christ. I didn't see Jesus walking down the streets in the physical sense this morning, but when I saw you walk in the door, I saw the body of Christ: because Jesus is sitting on the right hand of the Father.

Now the Holy Spirit is present, and Jesus is working in our heart, but we're the ones who have to carry out His work on the earth. Through the power of the Holy Spirit we can do it. So we have this ministry. Secondly, we have this ministry, this treasure, in earthen vessels.

Confident in Jesus

Thirdly, it's for this cause that we faint not. We are confident with the ministry of God. Because we know that God raised Jesus from the dead, we are also confident that Jesus can raise us out of the problems we're going through. If God raised Jesus from the dead, then Jesus can bring us out of the hell that we're going through right now. If God can raise Jesus from the dead, then He can pull you out of the financial predicament that you're in right now. If God could raise Jesus from the dead, than He can pull you out of that bad relationship that you're in right now.

This is a holistic message of the gospel that we've got to promote. This is what this quest for spiritual renewal is all about. We cannot let our salvation be in vain. There have been too many prayer meetings, there have been too many Bible studies and we've spent too much time on our knees to let this thing be in vain. But it's not over till it's over. There is some more gospel to be preached, more souls to be saved.

Press On

Don't be discouraged. There might be some preacher who has backslidden, or some deacon or maybe some trustee, or choir member, or someone who used to come and sit down in the pew faithfully and praise God. Now their church is the liquor house. Oh, but don't you be discouraged. You press on and serve God. If the preacher doesn't serve God, you serve God. If the people don't serve God, or if a trustee, or if a choir member, if a member of the congregation doesn't serve Him, you serve Him. You seek out your own soul salvation with fear and trembling, because we're all going to have to stand before the judgment throne for ourselves.

A Constant Pursuit

The quest, the search, the pursuit, the mission, the journey for spiritual renewal.... First, we've looked at this ministry that we've got. Second, we know that this ministry is a treasure in earthen vessels. But thirdly, the Word says in the 16th chapter, "For which cause we faint not, but though our outward man perish, yet our inward man is renewed day by day."

This quest for spiritual renewal is not something that can just happen Sunday morning. As I said before, it can't happen just on Monday night, or Wednesday night, but it must happen day by day. That means in this quest for spiritual renewal, this walk with God, that we've got to walk with Him in good times, we've got to walk with Him in bad times. We must walk with the Lord, because God is our healer, God is our deliverer, God is our way and we must keep our confession.

We must keep our faith even in the most difficult times, because there is somebody who's looking at our lives, that God wants to pull out. There is somebody who is on drugs, somebody who is on crack, or somebody who just didn't want to be bothered with God. But through our life, through our consistency, they will be touched. Their lives will be changed. They will come to the altar. They will be saved. They will be motivated and their lives will be changed.

Stand on God's Word

Though this outward man perishes, though we get to the point where our health may begin to dim, we still must stand on God's Word. Though we come across times of great persecution, we must stand on God's Word. Paul put it like this: "We are troubled on every side, but yet not distressed."

Trouble will come in your life, but you can have trouble without being distressed. You can go through trouble if you have God in your life and not experience distress, because you know that God has given you a vision. And for every vision that

God gives, He will give provision, and He will make a way, He will open up a door.

Chapter 11

STIR UP THE GIFT WITHIN - THE RESULT OF REAL REVIVAL

The Written Word

Second Timothy the 1st chapter, verses 1 through 7 reads, "Paul, an apostle of Jesus Christ by the will of God, according to the promise of life which is in Christ Jesus, to Timothy my dearly beloved son, grace, mercy and peace from God the Father, and from Christ Jesus our Lord. I thank God, whom I serve from my forefathers with a pure conscience, that without ceasing I have remembrance of thee in my prayers night and day, greatly desiring to see thee, being mindful of thy tears, that I may be filled with joy.

"When I call to remembrance the unfeigned faith that is in thee, which dwelt first in my grandmother Lois, and thy mother Eunice; and I am persuaded that in thee also. Wherefore I put thee in remembrance that thou stir up the gift of God, which is in thee by the putting on of my hands. For God hath not given us the spirit of fear, but of power, and of love, and of a sound mind."

I'd like to share from the following subject: "Stir up the Gift of God."

This book of 2nd Timothy is a letter from the apostle Paul to his son in the ministry. Timothy is one of the first young pastors in the church of our Lord and Savior, Jesus Christ. God has accomplished a marvelous work in this young man's life. And Paul has stepped out to be a father to Timothy.

A Father In Ministry

In our walk with the Lord, we need fathers in ministry. A father in the ministry is a pastor who watches out for your soul; he makes sure that you are spiritually equipped with the Word of God. He or she knows that Satan will try to come against you, so in his teaching, and in his preaching, he makes sure that he equips you with the things that you need to overcome the devil.

When Paul greets this young pastor by the name of Timothy, one of the first things I want you to notice is that he greets him with three words: grace, mercy and peace.

Now Paul only uses this greeting of grace, mercy and peace when he writes to the pastors. When he writes to the churches, you'll notice in the letters to the church he will say, "Grace and mercy." But when he writes to the pastors, such as Timothy, and Titus he says, "Grace, mercy and peace." He realized that these pastors needed the peace of God to prevail in their lives, because there were problems that were going on in dealing with the people.

The Role of a Leader

And that drives home the point that as Christians, we must learn that not only must the pastor stir up the gift of God within him, but members of the church must also, individually and collectively, stir up the gift of God within them.

God has a gift that He has given unto you. God has a calling that is also upon your life, and God wants you to fulfill that gift. He wants you to fulfill that calling upon your life.

The book of Timothy, especially 2nd Timothy, is mandatory reading for all pastors, but it's also mandatory reading for all Christians who are serious about the work of the Lord. And not only about the work of the Lord, but who are serious about the Lord of revival, or the Lord of the work.

It's not a book for those who want to be lightweights in the gospel. It's not a book for those who don't want to make an impact on society. But, for those who want to make a difference, to bring about a change in the society in which we live, it tells us how to stir up the gift of God within us.

A Gift To Remember

Now I want to talk about this gift, because the Bible says in Proverbs the 18th chapter, and the 16th verse that a man's gift will make room for him, and bring him before great men. That word there is *Mattan* in that scripture. "Mattan" means a present a gift, something to give, a reward. There is a gift, a present that God has given to you, and God wants you to share that gift with someone else.

When I was at Christ Chapel headquarters in Nigeria, coming back from one of the services, I saw some of the young men drawing signs and banners they were going to hang up for the meeting. Instantly, in my spirit, I thought about that scripture, that a man's gift will make room for him, and bring him before great men. We must present our God-given talents, skills and abilities as gifts unto the Lord.

Those young men and young women were drawing the signs, and they were utilizing their artistic skills, talents, and abilities as a gift unto the Lord.

Singers minister through music, using their talents, skills and abilities as a gift for the kingdom of God.

A Feast for the Palette

I was talking with my brothers after dinner and I shared with them that the food was so good in Africa. It was so good that it makes your tongue rise up and slap your brains out. The men and women who prepared the food used their cooking talents, skills, and abilities as gifts unto God. Everybody doesn't have the gift to cook that type of good food. Therefore, they cannot present it as a gift. You taste some food that somebody else prepared, and you want to push the plate away. But when they have the skills, talents and abilities to cook, they've got an anointing to cook. Not only will your soul be blessed, but your stomach will be blessed and your taste buds will be blessed.

So we're talking about stirring up the gift of God that is within you. Let me break it down a little further. My Pastor, the late Rev. Arthur L. Mackey, Sr., Pastor Emeritus of Mount Sinai Baptist Church, in Roosevelt, New York, would always prepare every year the Pastor's stew. He would get a big pot, and he would put potatoes, and onions, and all type of meat, and the best sauce, and carrots, and string beans, and a little of this, and a little of that, and he would have the fire low. He said, "Don't turn up the fire too high, because we don't want it to burn at the bottom, because if it burns at the bottom, and you begin to stir it, it will give it a bad taste and nobody will want to come back and get anymore."

So, there was a young man who would always stand at the pot and stir the stew, and that young man is preaching to you tonight. I would stand there and stir that pot of stew. And in my spirit God was showing me that we have to stir up the gift of God that is within us.

The Main Ingredient

Within us there is not just potatoes, string beans, and different types of meat. But there are callings and gifts that God has placed in this congregation. We have to stir it up. We cannot put all of the responsibility upon the pastor. The pastor must share the vision, but we must go out and make that vision a reality. We must go forth and take the Word that God has given us and apply it to real life situations. We must apply it to the real hard times in which we live, apply it to the situations of our present predicament and our present existence.

So I just want everybody right now to stand on their feet and imagine that your spirit is like that pot of stew, amen. And you take that spoon, you take that handle and begin to turn it. You stir up the gift of God that's within you. Take both of your hands and put them out like this. And begin to stir up the gift of God within you.

He may have given you a gift to be able to teach, or preach, sing, witness, draw, write, counsel, run, dance, work with children, work with married couples, work with divorced couples or to work with bereavement groups. But, whatever the gift is, whatever it is that God showed you in the midnight hour, whatever it is that God showed you in the weak times, whatever it was that God showed you in the wee hours of the morning, I want you to stir up that gift within you, stir up that anointing. Don't let it burn up, because the fire is burning, don't let it burn up. But stir it up, keep it flowing, keep it growing, keep it going for Jesus.

God Wants To Use You

Don't let that gift stay there dormant. God wants to use you. He wants to use your voice to sing with. He wants to use your voice to witness with. He wants to use your hands to prepare meals. He wants to use your head to draw great signs and great murals. Oh, He wants to use your hand to make great statues, not a monument unto man, not a statute to worship Him but something to display the gospel of Jesus Christ.

He wants you to stir up the gift, the gift that is in you. Hallelujah. Give God the praise and glory. Thank you, Jesus, thank you Jesus.

A Spiritual Assignment

As we look at that verse, pick up your Bibles. In 2nd Timothy, we realize that Paul has a spiritual assignment from God. That spiritual assignment is to help Timothy remember. "Sometimes you've got to remember where God has brought you from."

Let's look at the Acts of the Apostles, the 16th chapter, and let's share a little bit about Timothy. In Acts the 16th chapter, it gives us some background about this young man: "Then came he to Derby and to Listra," talking about the apostle Paul. "And behold a certain disciple…". So we know that before Timothy became a great pastor, he was a disciple. He was a follower of Christ. So many folk want to get in the big positions, but the way to go up in Christ is to go down on your knees, to be a servant.

It says that, "he was a disciple named Timothus… the son of a certain woman who was a Jewess, and believed she was a Christian." She was a Christian Jew. "But his father was a Greek." So, we have a problem here. Knowing Timothy is a disciple, many of the Christians who were also Jews did not want to accept him because his father was Greek. This was an interracial child and some folks had problems with this mixed child coming in, trying to do the work of the Lord. There was a racism of sorts. There was discrimination of sorts that was occurring, both in the physical, and in the religious sense.

Nationality Doesn't Make a Difference

In the 2nd verse it says, "Which was well reported." Talking about his father being a Greek, it should not have mattered at all, but it did matter in the hearts and minds of many men and women that really didn't have themselves right with God. "Which was well reported by the brethren that were in Listra in Iconium. Him would Paul have to go forth with him, and took and circumcised him," talking about Timothy, "because of the Jews which were in those quarters, for they all knew that his father was a Greek."

So, Paul said in essence, instead of me fussing with everybody, I'm just going to take Timothy to be circumcised, because the gospel has got to be preached to everybody, whether they are Jew or a Greek. In order for the gift of God to be stirred up in us, there are some things that we have to circumcise. There are some things that we have to cut off. And there are some things that we have to allow God to cut away. It might hurt, it will be painful, but then the gift can come forth.

201

Cut It Off

Sometimes we cannot stir up the gift because there is something in the way of the gift. Sometimes we can't stir up the gift, because there is something blocking the gift. But God is calling us to allow Him to circumcise us. And whatever it is that's holding us back from utilizing the gift that God has given to us, He's saying, "Let Me cut it off. Let Me remove it right now." No matter what it is, whether it's addiction to drugs, God is saying, "Let Me cut it off right now. Let Me circumcise it right now."

Or, whether it is a dependence upon alcohol, God is saying, "Let Me cut it off right now. Let Me circumcise it, so the gift might truly come forth."

Whether it is, you feel like you just can't stop cussing, or lying, or cheating, or stealing but God wants to cut it off. He wants to circumcise it, so the gift might come forth in its fullness.

Let's go back to 2nd Timothy. Now we realize some of the discrimination that Timothy was up against, and the fact that folk didn't really want to accept him. When he went to the Corinthian church, Paul constantly had to write the Corinthians and tell them to accept and to receive Timothy, "my son in the ministry."

Pray for Each Other

God sometimes will give you a gift, but many may not want to accept it. If God has given you a gift, you must realize that that gift will revolutionize somebody's life, and that you never can give up on the gift that God has given unto you.

So God calls Timothy to remembrance through his father in the ministry, the apostle Paul. He says in the 3rd verse, "I thank God whom I serve for my forefathers." This is the apostle Paul talking, and "with a pure conscience, that without ceasing I have." I have what? "Remembrance of thee in my prayers night and day."

We have to remember to pray for each other night and day. You must pray for your pastor, night and day. You must pray for your brother, and your sister, your mother, your father, every relative, every neighbor, night and day. We take prayer too lightly. God can transform lives through the power of prayer. Prayer is communication with God. Prayer is not just us talking to God, but prayer is also listening, and hearing the voice of the Father. Pray, and let Him speak to your heart. Pray, and let Him minister to your soul. Pray, and let Him revive your life, because that is one of the first steps in learning how to stir up the gift. We can say, "Stir up the gift of God within you," but somebody might say, "Rev. Mackey, Jr. how do I stir up the gift?"

Committed to the Cause

First, you must remember to pray. You must have a life committed to prayer. One must not take prayer lightly, but be serious about prayer, and realize that God is not a being that we talk about. He is an everlasting God, He is an awesome God, and He is the Almighty God who can transform our lives.

So secondly, not only must we remember to pray but Paul goes on in the 4th verse saying, "Greatly desiring to see thee, and being mindful of thy tears." He knew that Timothy would pray and he would cry. All of the hardships that he was experiencing, Paul had to tell him, "Grace, mercy and peace." Also, Paul spoke the peace of God in life. In the midst of his tears, and in the midst of his struggles, Paul realized what was going on in Timothy's life. He said that you've got to remember where God has brought you from, that you may be filled with joy.

Filling the Void

"When I call to remembrance the unfeigned faith that is in thee which dwelt first in thy grandmother Lois." Listen to this, "And in thy mother Eunice, and I am persuaded that in thee also."

203

But he doesn't mention his father the Greek. This is many years later, after the scripture that we read in Acts. Maybe his father is dead, I don't know. But I do know that the scripture clearly lets us know that in the 2nd verse Paul calls him "Timothy, my dearly beloved son." And I want to let you know, that whatever is missing in your life, God will fill that void. There may be someone who has lost a child, someone who has experienced a divorce, someone whose mother or father is gone. There's a void that is in your life, but I'm here to let you know that God, through His awesome presence and power, will fill that void. There is no one who will ever be your mother, there is no one that will ever be your father, and there is no one that will ever be your son, or be your daughter. Only God can fill that void in your life.

And what God wants to do is fill that void with the gift that He has placed in you. Because as you utilize that gift, you're utilizing the training that you got from your mother, or from your father. And if they were a Christian, you're utilizing the training, even far greater than that which God has already placed in your life. God is calling us to stir up the gift that is within us, He's calling us to stir up that gift that will fill the void that is in our lives.

A Rich Heritage

The 5th verse says, "I call to remembrance that unfeigned faith." So Paul, in that verse, is calling us to remember our heritage of faith. Not only does he call us first of all to pray, because prayer is one of the foundations of revival, but he's calling us to remember our heritage, our rich heritage of faith. That is another way that we stir up the gift of God within us by remembering to pray. And then by remembering our rich heritage of faith; to realize that the church is much bigger than we realize, that there are brothers and sisters all across Africa who are worshipping God in spirit and in truth.

There are brothers and sisters all across America who are worshipping God in spirit and in truth. There are brothers and sisters all across Asia, all across Europe and all across India who are worshipping God in spirit and in truth. But not only that, the church also includes the dead in Christ. Oh, it also includes Paul and Timothy, it includes Matthew, Mark, Luke and John. But not only that, it includes those in the New Testament church who died in the faith. This includes the Old Testament believers as well. The prophets like Elijah, Isaiah, Habakkuk, Nahum, Zephaniah, and saints like Moses and David are all a part of God's glorious church.

So when we begin to look at our rich Christian heritage, we realize it includes great men and women of God throughout the world in every walk of life. And I realize that we have a family. I'm not in this thing alone. Not only am I called to stir up the gift of God within me, but also I am supposed to stir my brothers and sisters in the ministry. God is calling us to stir up the gift of God within us.

So the first point is to remember to pray, if you want to stir up the gift of God.

The second point is to remember your rich Christian heritage of faith, if you want to stir up the gift of God within you.

Don't Forget

Look at the 6th verse. It says, "Wherefore I put thee in" what? "Remember to stir up the gift of God." It means that someone else's spirit will begin to catch on fire. As their spirit and their soul begins to catch on fire, and they feel the presence of the Holy Ghost moving all over them, they'll begin to stir up the gift of God. They'll stir up the calling of God. And realize deep down within them, the fact that they're chosen by God.

The fire of the Holy Spirit moves and it touches one, and it touches another, then it touches another, and it touches another, and it begins to spread like wild fire.

The Holy Spirit Can't Be Controlled

Rev. Bernice A. King, daughter of the late civil rights leader Rev. Dr. Martin Luther King, Jr., said that "The Holy Spirit cannot be controlled by us; instead, the Holy Spirit controls us. When something controls us, it means something has gotten deep inside us. That's why all throughout the book of Acts, it says that the Apostles were filled with the Holy Spirit, not that they *had* the Holy Spirit. When you're filled with the Holy Spirit, no problem is too difficult to handle, no burden too difficult to bear, no illness too difficult to heal. That's why we can have the Holy Spirit and still not have real power. But when we are filled with the Holy Spirit, we have power that can take on the world." [1]

Burn It Up

Have you ever seen a tree when it is dry and begins to catch on fire? Then another tree is ignited and flames begin to spread through the forest like wild fire. They don't know how to stop it from consuming all of the grass, and it's consuming all of the tress. My Bible tells me that our God is a consuming fire. That's what God wants us to do. In fact, that's what it means when we look at that Word. When we look at that Word, the gift, in 2nd Timothy 1:6 it means to snatch. It means to terminate, it means to consume. God wants to give you a gift that will consume you. God wants to give you a gift that will burn up everything that is not holy in your life. God wants to give you a gift that will burn up everything that's not right in your life. God wants to give you a gift for everything that's not righteous in your life.

There's a Purpose for the Gift

God gives you this gift and this gift's purpose is to consume everything that's not right in you, to purge it out, to purify you, to bring sanctification into your life. So if God has called you to sing, while singing give God all the praise. Brother, as you play those drums, as you work on those tapes, stir up the gift. Day by day, as you stir up the gift within you, it consumes you. It puts a deep desire in you to serve Him even more.

Now since you're using your gift, it consumes you. You've got your mind on the things of God. You've got your mind on the work of the ministry. You might be making the food, but as you make the food, you realize that you're ministering. As you prepare the juice, you realize that you're ministering. As you drive the van, you realize that you're ministering. As you carry the pastor's briefcase, you realize that you're ministering. As you go out on the streets and witness to somebody, you realize that you're ministering. You're stirring up the gift of God within you.

Abide in the Gift

You've got the gifts, because God laid His hands on you. You could have been avoided, you could have died, but you're here right now. You've got to stir up that gift. You've got to use that gift. Your gift will make room for you. Your gift will kick doors down for you, and your gift will consume you. Anything that's not right it will burn it up, if you just use the gift, if you flow in the anointing, if you walk in your calling, if you realize that you're chosen by God; you have stirred up the gift. Glory to you, God.

If you don't stir up the gift of God within you, that gift which actually means in the Greek to consume, as our God is a consuming fire, if you don't fan the flame, and experience the flame of God's Spirit; you're going to experience a flame, all right, but it will be to lift your eyes up in hell, in eternal torment.

Tell Someone About Jesus

So God is saying, instead of going that route, "Let My consuming fire move in your life." "For God so loved the world that He gave His only begotten Son that whosoever believeth in Him should not perish but have everlasting life."

There's somebody who might feel discouraged because, "I don't know what my gift is. I don't know what to use for the kingdom of God."

If you've got Jesus, you've got the best gift of all. If you just go and tell folk about Jesus, you'll be using your gift.

There may be one who wants to receive this gift, wants to receive this present that God has given, the Lamb that was slain before the foundations of the earth was laid. Tell that person about Jesus. There may be somebody who wants to get right with God. Share this scripture, "If you deny Me before men, then I will deny you before My Father which is in heaven. But if you confess Me before men, I will confess you before My Father which is in heaven."

Pray that God would heal people everywhere. The scripture says that God is a God who is able to heal. "He was wounded for our transgressions, He was bruised for our iniquities, the chastisement of His peace was upon us, and with His stripes we are healed."

Divine Healing

I want you to focus on two things: the Lord has given you a gift and He wants you to use it. God has the power to heal whatever is going on in your life right now, whether it's a problem on the inside, or a problem on the outside. Whatever the situation is, believe right now. Focus on the fact that Jesus has already paid it all. On Calvary's old rugged cross He said, "It is finished." And when He said that, and He gave up the ghost, and He rose from the dead, your healing was made complete.

The Gift Belongs to Me for Ministry

Remember to take back what the devil has stolen. Reach out and take it by force. Say, "I take it back. What the devil has stolen from me," reach out and grab it, reach out and grab it. It's not just for one thing. There are other things that I'm taking back that the devil has stolen from me. I've got some family members that are not saved; I'm taking back what the devil stole from me. A young man who's on drugs; I'm taking him back. The young woman on the corner; I'm taking her back. Someone despised me, someone rejected me, someone disinherited me, but I'm taking it back and we're not taking no mess off the devil. Devil, you've stolen too much, but we're taking back our territory. We're taking back Nigeria, Africa, America, our homes, our families, our sons, our community, our daughters; we boldly pull down spiritual strongholds. We pull down oppression. We pull down demon possession, negative influence, lies, generational curses, we pull it down. We break it, we destroy it in the spirit with the gift that God has given to us.

The kingdom of God suffereth violence, but the violent take it by force. Oh, we've got to take it by force. We're going to take the territory that God gave us. We're going to take and use this gift, and tell Satan, "Satan, this means war!"

When God lays His hands upon us, and we begin to stir up the gift that's within us, we will realize, as verse 7 says, "God has not given us the spirit of fear, but of power, and of love, and of a sound mind."

Someone was fearful to use their gift. I'm sure you said, "What would someone else think if I share what God has given to me?" But God is saying, stir it up. Put it to use, because it will make a difference in Africa, and it will make a difference in the world.

Chapter 12

THE GLORY OF THE LATTER HOUSE - CONSIDER YOUR WAYS

A True Prophet

In this study concerning Real Revival I call your attention to the Old Testament book of Haggai. Haggai is considered a minor prophet but he has a message relevant to the church today, a major message. The reason why he's called a minor prophet is because he foretold the things that God shared with him after the exile, after the Jewish people were held captive in Babylon by king Nebuchadnezzar. There are several prophets. Sixteen in all in the Old Testament. Eleven of them prophesied before King Nebuchadnezzar took the Jewish people into captivity, into slavery, into bondage. Those 11 were Ezra, Nehemiah, Isaiah, Jeremiah (and Lamentations, which was written by Jeremiah), Hosea, Joel, Amos, Nahum, Habakkuk and Zephaniah. So they prophesied before the exile, before captivity in Babylon with Nebuchadnezzar.

And during the exile, there was preaching and prophesying from the likes of Ezekiel and Daniel. The experiences of Daniel and the story about the three Hebrew boys in the fiery furnace, all happened during the captivity in Babylon.

But after that period of bondage in the Jewish people's lives, Haggai, Zechariah and Malachi were the last three prophets to prophesy in the name of the Lord. One of the reasons why the book of Haggai is so short is that he only prophesied for four months. That is one thing that we must understand. God has a purpose for everyone. We must move in God's timing. If it is only meant for you to get up once and share a Word from the

Lord, then you want to please God for that one time, or because you are moving in God's purpose, to do His will and make a difference in somebody's life.

Go Forth

So he only prophesied for a period of four months--the months of August and September, and then in December and January of the year BC 520. During this time, the Chinese philosopher Confucius was coming into prominence. But the Lord didn't want to deal with that mass confusion, God wanted to give a message that was physically clear to the people.

At this time when Confucius was expounding his philosophies in China, God raised up Haggai to bring forth a word from the Lord to the Jewish people. This word was going forth, as God designed it to.

So we want to look at Haggai, the 2nd chapter, verses 1 through 9. It says, "Speak now to Zerubbabel the son of Shealtiel, governor of Judah, and to Joshua the son of Josedech, the high priest, and to the residue of the people, saying, Who is left among you that saw this house in her first glory? And how do you see it now? is it not in your eyes in comparison of it as nothing?"

"Yet now be strong, oh Zerubbabel, saith the Lord; and be strong, oh Joshua, son of Josedech, the high priest; and be strong, all ye people of the land, saith the Lord, and work; for I am with you, saith the Lord of hosts. According to the word that I covenanted with you when ye came out of Egypt, so my spirit remaineth among you; fear ye not."

"For thus saith the Lord of hosts; Yet once, it is a little while, and I will shake the heavens, and the earth, and the sea, and the dry land; and I will shake all nations, and the desire of all nations shall come; and I will fill this house with glory, saith the Lord of hosts. The silver is Mine, and the gold is Mine, saith the Lord of hosts. The glory of this latter house shall be greater than that of the former, saith the Lord of hosts; and in this place will I give peace, saith the Lord of hosts."

Setting Your Priorities Straight

Let's look at the 9th verse. It says, "The glory of this latter house.... The glory of this latter house." And I would like to share a supporting subject as well, "putting our priorities in place."

The glory of the latter house; putting our priorities in place. Haggai's name means, "to peace". Haggai had one purpose in life and that was to encourage and motivate the Jewish people to build the temple after the exile. It's between 15 to 18 years after the Jewish people flee Babylonian captivity under Nebuchadnezzar. And during the preaching of Nehemiah, he encouraged them to rebuild the walls. He also encouraged them to build the temple, but they did not finish that work.

Zerubbabel led them out of captivity and the governor of Jerusalem brought them back into their home land. God laid it on their hearts to build this temple. But they became preoccupied with their own lives. It is true that we worship together. We like to think about our corporate destiny. We are one body in Christ, but also we are individual Christians and we have our personal destiny. Personally, we take care of things in our home, we provide for our home, we put food on the table and do the things that we must do. More importantly, God wants us to do for our family, the Bible says if a man doesn't work he should not eat. So when we take care of our homes, our jobs and family were nurturing our personal destiny. And our corporate destiny is when we embrace our church family, as one in the body of Christ.

The Point of Power

In the book of Haggai, God makes it very clear about the importance of corporate destiny. Our personal relationship with the Lord is the launching pad for corporate destiny. We must have that personal relationship with God. We must know Him for ourselves first, and then as we come together we should agree. But the most important thing is to agree. The point of power is agreement.

If we are in disagreement there is no power. When the 120 came together in the upper room, they were on one accord, then the Spirit of God came down like a rushing mighty wind.

The Lord of Hosts

So when we look in the book of Haggai the 1st chapter, it says, "In the second year of Darius the king, in the sixth month, in the first day of the month, came the word of the Lord by Haggai the prophet unto Zerubbabel the son of Shealtiel, governor of Judah, and to Joshua the son of Josedech, the high priest, saying, "Thus speaketh the Lord of hosts, saying, This people say, The time is not come, the time that the Lord's house should be built. Then came the word of the Lord by Haggai the prophet, saying, Is it time for you, oh ye, to dwell in your cieled houses, your elaborate house, in this house, and this house lie waste? Now therefore, thus saith the Lord of hosts."

That's a very interesting term, the Lord of hosts. It means the Lord with a massive persona. *Tsaba* is the word in the Hebrew. *Tsaba*, a massive person organized for war, the lord of an army. The lord of a campaign, the lord of a battle, the lord of a company of soldiers. So when it says "The Lord of hosts," it's talking about the church as being soldiers. A mass group of believers baptized in the Name of Jesus and washed in the blood of the Lamb.

A Fresh Word from the Lord

"The Lord of hosts, saying, Consider your ways." That's the first point we must realize in this message about the glory of the latter house; and putting our priorities in place.

The Lord woke me up early in the morning, and He said "Haggai, Haggai," and I opened up Haggai, and the first three words I read were "Consider your ways." That jumped out at me.

I said, "Lord, I'm not in any gross sin. What are you saying?"

He said, "Consider your ways." Jesus said it like this, "Let a man examine himself, so let him eat of this bread, and let him drink of this cup, so that he can discern the Lord's body.

So we must examine ourselves, we must consider our ways. There is one thing about God: if something is not right, He knows how to block the blessings. It doesn't sound nice, and it steps on our feet. "Step on my feet, Jesus." I want the Word to convict me. Because when people don't let the Word convict them, they end up in scandal. They end up in a mess. But when you let the Word step on you, it brings integrity into your life. It keeps you on the straight and narrow. So we all want the Word of God to come into our lives and convict us and clean up whatever mess is going on.

So, He challenged them to consider their ways. The children of Israel, the Jewish people of this time, were told by God to build a temple. Many years passed by and they had not completed the work. And God said to them, "Consider your ways." You're concerned about your own homes you're concerned about making them elaborate and comfortable to live in.

Consider Your Ways

God understands our needs, He understands that we need to have a roof above our head, food to eat and some type of structure in our lives.

But yet He says "Consider your ways." And so this isn't so much an indictment upon any gross sins, but "consider your ways" applies to everything. Any form of disobedience is sin, whether it's a little lie or a big one. People say I told "a little white lie, or a big black lie"--that's foolishness. Any form of disobedience, any form of missing the mark, is sin. So "All have sinned and fallen short of the glory of God." But that's the reason why we must stay connected and hooked up with Jesus. We don't have to live a life of sin, we don't have to be controlled by sin. We can allow the Spirit to work through us and prevail.

Go down in the 6th verse. It says, "Ye have sown much, and bring in little; ye eat, but ye have not enough; ye drink, but ye are not filled with drink; ye clothe you, but there is none warm; and he that earneth wages earneth wages to put it into a bag with holes." Seems like you never can get ahead, one problem after the next, one burden, one heartache after the next. When you're going through hard times, consider this saying: "When circumstances press hard against you, do not push them away."

Self Examination Is Important

It is the potter's hand. He is shaping you into a vessel of beauty and honor." God is saying is, "Consider your ways." If you want to flow in the glory of the latter house, and learn how to put your priorities straight, well the first thing has to do with considering your ways. You must examine yourself. Socrates said that the unexamined life is not worth living. But I liked it better when Jesus said, "Let a man examine himself."

"Let a man, let a woman," examine themselves, "and so let them eat of this bread and let them drink of this cup. Let them understand the suffering that Jesus fights with, for the church and that He died for us.

And then the Bible says, "Husbands, love your wives as Christ loved the church." What does that mean? That means if Christ laid down His life for the church of God, then you lay down your life for your wife. You've got to lay down your life for your family. You've got to put your life on the line, but that's what leadership is all about.

Men say, "I want to be a leader, I want to step out in the front."

That means you're ready to die. That means you're ready to put down your life. That's what leadership is all about.

So Haggai tells them "Consider your ways," but also he lets them know that one of the reasons why they're going through the things that they're going through is that they have not put their priorities right. It hurts when you have to do what God tells you to do. Sometimes we want to put our money somewhere else, we want to invest somewhere else, we want to do our own thing, we want to do what is right for us; and that's only natural. It's only human to feel that way.

But yet God is telling us to put our priorities straight because He wants us to experience the glory of the latter house.

Victorious Over Disobedience

Not only does He tell them to consider their ways in reference to not building the temple, but He points out that the reason why they are suffering is directly related to their disobedience. Let me bring this point out. For example, if a person is sleeping around, lying, bickering, gossiping, and backbiting, God will shut up some blessings, especially in the local church.

So when we become part of the local fellowship we've got to watch what we do. We have to watch how we carry ourselves. Although we are members of a church, we are members of the body of Christ. And it is scriptural. If there is sin in the camp, God will block blessing corporately, but yet there might be individual blessings in your own life. And then sometimes folk gather together with other wicked people, and they call it blessings, but it's not really blessings. It's just wicked people who used a whole bunch of wicked money for the wrong purposes and it looks like they're blessed. But they're not. So he goes on and says, "Not only do I want you to consider your ways, but I want you to be strong in work." That's the second point. But about that first point, "Consider your ways." The thing that really brings this point home is found in the 12th verse. It says, "Then Zerubbabel, the son of Shealtiel, and Joseph the son of Josedech, the high priest, with all the remnant of the people...." These were poor people. A lot of the rich people who lived comfortably remained in Babylon. They were in captivity, but they realized that Nebuchadnezzar had a lot of money, and a lot of gold. Nevertheless, they wanted to stick around even if they were freed from captivity. They had their freedom in terms of more people, and they stayed there.

Captivity vs. Freedom

So, the ones that returned to Jerusalem and Judah, were poor folk, the remnant. But these poor people had a love for God. Speaking of captivity and freedom, I often think about the slaves of America and how they built church after church regardless of how many times they were burned to the ground. I went riding in the area about 20 or 30 miles out. Suddenly, I saw beautiful lights and lot of cars In the midst was a beautiful church building. Many of these churches were built during slavery or after slavery, but how did they get the money to do this?

They had a mind to work. They had very little money or none at all. Today, we've got all types of money. We've got all types of resources, and we can't do half the things that they did back then. It's the philosophy of how you look at things.

When God Speaks

So it says that, "The remnant of all the people obeyed the voice of the Lord their God." See, the source of power is in agreement. It is important to listen to the man or woman of God, because God speaks through His servants. You can't do your own thing. We must be sensitive to the move of the Lord.

When God spoke to Moses, the voice of God sounded like Moses. And God, when He spoke to Paul, sounded like Paul. God uses men, and God uses women. We have to have an attentive ear to hear when God is speaking. "He that hath an ear, let him hear what the Spirit saith to the churches."

217

The words of the prophet Haggai: "The Lord their God has sent him, and the people did fear before the Lord." They have a respect, they have a reverence. "Then spake Haggai the Lord's messenger."

So not only was Haggai the Lord's messenger, he was also in the Lord's message. You know how you talk about being in the will of God? He was in the sermon, he was in the message, and he was in the proclamation. When Haggai spoke, it was synonymous with God speaking, because God was speaking through the prophet. He surrendered to God, and he was God's mouthpiece. The people respected that and they were in agreement. As we previously discussed, agreement is the place of what? Power.

So we're talking about the glory of the latter house, putting our priorities in place. "And the Lord stirred the spirit of Zerubbabel the son of Shealtiel, governor of Judah, and the spirit of Joshua the son of Josedech, the high priest, and the spirit of all the remnant of the people. And they came and did work in the house of the Lord of hosts, their God."

Stirred by the Word

When they heard the message, their spirits were stirred by what God had said. There's a time, when we must "Stir up the gift within us." But then there is also a time, when God stirs us through His Word.

We've got to get stirred up in the Lord, so we can experience the glory of the latter house. We've got to get stirred up in God so we can put our priorities straight. We've got to get stirred up by God, so we won't go on with business as usual. I'm not going back to Egypt, I'm not going back to Babylon, I'm not going back to slavery, and I'm not going back to captivity. Thank you, Jesus. Lord, give us understanding.

Let's look in the 2nd chapter. In order to experience the glory of the latter house, in order to put our priorities straight, we must first consider our ways and examine ourselves. Secondly, we must be strong in the Word.

In the 2nd chapter verse 2 it says, "Speak now to Zerubbabel the son of Shealtiel, governor of Judah, to Joshua the son of Josedech, the high priest, and to the residue of the people who is left among you who saw this house in her first glory." "First glory."

The Lord Is Not Through Blessing

"And how do you see it now? Is it not in your eyes in comparison of it as nothing?"

One of the worst things that can happen is when someone prejudges the work of God based on the move of God they've experienced in the past. Paul says, "Forgetting those things which are behind I press towards the mark for the prize of the high calling of God in Christ Jesus." Of course, that is a balanced message, you know. It's a balanced message to look back at your old landmark. The same Bible that says "Let us look back to the old landmark," is the same Bible that says, "Behold, I will do a new work, and I will make a way in the wilderness."

And so we have to get a balance between what God is saying. There are references in the scripture concerning Egypt, and the Lord wants us to draw strength and motivation from what He has already done for us. But yet, He really wants us to realize that there are better days ahead. We must have this balance which is clearly described in the scriptures. Yes, the Lord has brought us from a mighty long way. And yes, there were great days in the past, but our greatest days, the church's greatest days are ahead.

Take a closer look at the scripture. There were many people who complained. They said, "We remember, we remember Solomon's temple." There was gold in the temple. It was elaborate and beautiful. People would come from all over the world to see the glory and splendor of Solomon's temple. So this temple could not even compare to what we've had, and the people became concerned. They already went through 18 years of discouragement and as they worked, they became discouraged again.

Godly Strength Is the Key

But God came in and stopped that foolishness. He says to them in the 14th verse through Haggai, "Yet now be strong." It's evident that this temple was nothing in comparison to what we had before. The scripture says, "But yet now be strong with Zerubbabel, saith the Lord, and be strong."

"Oh Joshua of Josedech, the high priest, be strong, all ye people of the land." It didn't say be strong and try to hold on, because that's not enough. But then it says "and work." So we've got to be strong. We have to have tenacity, and as Dr. A.R. Bernard says, "we have to be persistent."

The reason why the door isn't open is because we stopped knocking. We've got to continue to knock, we've got to continue to work, and we've got to be persistent. We've got to be strong. We've got to remember that 18 years prior to this, Nehemiah preached "for the joy of the Lord is your strength."

We've also got to be consistent. When they heard that message Nehemiah preached, they began to build the temple, but they didn't finish it. It wasn't enough to realize that He was their strength. In contrast, believers have to stand sure, knowing that God is our strength. And because He is the personification of strength, I'm going to work. And the blessings shall come to pass. Faith without works is dead.

Work Is Honorable

So the Word of the Lord goes on and says, "And work, for I am with you." He says, "Lo I am with you always until the end of the world," and if it's church work, do it. If God has called us to work in the service of God, say yes, Lord. Initially God has

220

called us to do so. We ought to be committed, and we ought to be strong in work.

If somebody has a religious spirit, pray for them. Somebody ain't acting right, pray for them. But you've got to be strong and work. You've heard the Word, you know the Word, so get the job done.

It goes on and says, "according to the Word that I covenanted with you when ye came out of Egypt," that being the covenant between His people, "so My Spirit remaineth among you, fear ye not."

In essence, God is saying: "You were in captivity in Egypt and in Babylon and I'm still with you. The promises that I gave to Abraham, Isaac, Jacob and Moses are still good today." All the promises of God are yea and amen.

Thirdly, he has already emphasized to "consider your ways," be strong in the work of God. You must do these things if you want to experience the glory of the latter house or reap the benefits of having your priorities straight.

A Divine Shake Up

And it goes on and says, "Thus saith the Lord of host, Yet once it is a little while and I will shake the heavens, and the sea, and the dry land." You see, until God gets what He wants, He'll allow hurricanes, earthquakes, floods, and all types of catastrophic disasters to happen, until we get ourselves in line with what He wants to do. He'll allow it.

So it goes on and says, that "The silver is Mine, and the gold is Mine." You're worried about building this temple, but all the resources are Mine. "The earth is the Lord's and the fullness thereof. The world disdains its will therein."

Put God First

We've got to tap into the source and we must be in agreement: don't try to push off our own philosophy, our own agenda, but get behind God's man. Get behind a pastor. Get behind the man that God has moved upon. Forget about your philosophies and humble yourself. It's easy. You might be saying, it's hard to respect the leadership that God gives. It's harder to hear the voice of the Lord through the man of God. But the scripture says that Haggai was the messenger of God, in the message, with the message.

You say, "Oh, that's the preacher. We don't want to respect the message." However, if we don't respect the message, or the one that God has sent the message through, God will not bless.

So He tells us to consider our ways. He tells us to be strong and work.

The Temple of God

You see, Solomon's temple was a beautiful temple, but Solomon had thousands of wives. And for all those thousands of wives that Solomon had, they all worshipped different gods. You want to know where they worshipped? In the temple where they were supposed to be worshipping Jehovah, where they were supposed to be worshipping the Lord their God.

The 9th verse says, "the glory of this latter house shall be greater than the former, saith the Lord of hosts. And in this place I will give peace, saith the Lord of hosts." God knew what He was talking about concerning the glory of the latter house.

Let's look ahead 500 years, in this same temple. A young boy about 12-years-old wanders away from his mother and father and goes into Solomon's temple and begins to read the scriptures. And mamma's looking around, "Where's my son? He's only 12. Where is my son?"

And they come into the temple and they see Him with the priests, and this young boy turns around and says, "Didn't you know that I'll be in My Father's house, about My Father's business." The glory of the latter house was greater than the former. That 12-year-old boy was Jesus Christ the Savior. They had to build that temple, so Jesus could go in there and read that scripture.

But not only that, when Jesus was about 30 years old, He went back into that temple up to the pulpit, and opened up the scripture, and preached His initial sermon He said, "The Spirit of the Lord is upon Me, because He has anointed Me to preach the gospel. To set at liberty them that are bruised, to preach the acceptable year of the Lord." He said, "This day is this prophecy fulfilled in your sight." The glory of the latter house was greater than the former, because Jesus was in the house.

Who Is in the House?

We've got to get our priorities straight. We've got to consider our ways. We've got to be strong in work, so Jesus can come into the house. He doesn't want to come into a filthy sinner. Oh, but He wants the Holy Spirit to work through us, because the Holy Spirit is the agent of holiness. Remember this: "Holiness is nothing less than conformity to the character of God."[26] Jerry Bridges stated.

In closing, this is going to come through the Holy Spirit. And when we receive Jesus, the agent of holiness comes in our life and sheds His love in our hearts. He's trying to bring holiness into our life. He's trying to make us whole. He's trying to make us complete. But we've got to consider our ways. We've got to give up our own agenda. We must put down our idols. We've got to be strong and work to experience the glory, the presence of God in the latter house.

A Heavenly Peace

Later, after Jesus preached that sermon, He went out preaching, healing the sick and casting out demons. He came back into that temple and saw the money changers in there, and He saw them gambling. He picked up a rod: everybody talks about Jesus turning the other cheek, but Jesus also knew how to fight. He knew how to stand up, He was no sissy. He picked up a rod, and began to hit the money changers and run them out of there. He said, "Didn't you know that My Father's house is a house of worship, and not a den of thieves?"

The glory of the latter house is greater than the former. But what does this mean to us? How does this apply to us? How does this apply to our lives individually, our personal destiny? How does this apply to our corporate destiny?

Well, the scripture clearly says, "In this place I will give peace..."

You may have experienced a lot of heartache and pain, but God wants you to experience the glory of the latter house. Or, you may have lost a job, but God still wants you to experience the glory of the latter house. You're going through thousands of tribulations and you don't know how you're going to make it, but God wants you to experience the glory of the latter house.

The scripture says that we are new creatures in Christ, that old things are passed away, behold all things are new. The scripture says that we are the temple of God. So we had our old house before we were saved. But we've got a new house now. We are the children of God.

A Divine Experience

The only reason we don't experience the glory of the latter house is because we don't consider our ways and do not use our strength and work. But when we consider our ways, when we're strong and we work for the Lord, we will experience the glory of the latter house. Jesus put it this way, He said, "Greater works than these shall ye do in My Name, because I go to be with My Father." We are endowed with the Holy Spirit, the presence of God and the glory of God; but now we can add to this the glory of the latter house. The glory of the latter house is in me. Now how do I know that?

Well, I looked at 1st John 4:4. It says, "Greater is He that is in me than he that is in the world." The glory of the latter house, the presence of God is in me. I've got news for you, it's in you too. If you'll just praise Him and stop being dignified. Lift up the Name of Jesus and you will experience the glory of the latter house.

God will give you peace. God will give you healing. God will give you deliverance. God will bring you through, and He'll do it right. But you have got to be like Jesus and be about the Father's business. Consider your ways, strong in work. Say, "I'm pressing on the upward way, new heights I'm gaining every day. Lord help me as I'm homeward bound, and plant my feet on higher ground."

Oh, the church's greatest days lie ahead, the church's destiny lies ahead. God, let your glory and presence fill this place. Fill every man, woman, boy and girl. Let us experience The Glory Of The Latter House.

Chapter 13

REAL REVIVAL IN TROUBLED TIMES

Psalm 138:7 states that, "Though I walk in the midst of trouble, thou wilt revive me: thou shalt stretch forth thine hand against the wrath of mine enemies, and thy right hand shall save me."

In June, 1999 my father, the Rev. Dr. Arthur L. Mackey, Sr., was diagnosed with colon cancer which spread to the liver. My father was the highly esteemed Pastor of the Mt. Sinai Baptist Church in Roosevelt, N.Y. where I now currently serve as Pastor. My father was also one of the founder's of the Nassau Council of Black Clergy, and the first African-American to serve as the President of the Nassau County Medical Center. Across the years I stood by his side in many troubled times. I remembered when he lost his job when I was just a boy growing up in New York. That was long before he got involved in government and his ministry brought him to meetings at town hall, the county seat of government, and the White House. When I was just a young boy growing up and my father lost his secular job, he would take me fishing with him every single day except Sunday. I did not realize back then that he had lost his job and fishing was our only way of getting food, but I sure do appreciate it now as I look at the little faces of my three children. As I reflect back on that example, I appreciate it because I did not realize back then as a child that many boys did not have a father around at all. The testimony of my father's life and his lasting legacy is real revival in troubled times.

His example of going fishing when he lost his job when I was young boy gives me godly courage not to give up when the troubles of life come my way. That fish was our family of five's dinner.

At the time of this writing, I am about to release the evangelism team that my late father and Pastor, my spiritual father in the ministry started just prior to his being diagnosed with colon cancer which spread to the liver. Even in his troubled times, he still wanted to go fishing spiritually. If he could not physically get up and fish himself, he would establish an evangelism team to be fishers of men to win lost souls to Christ.

At the time of this writing, our church is planning for our first soul winning conference. Dad could not take us fishing as he did when I was just a young lad growing up in the church, but now as he lay in a hospital bed in pain and agony he asked me to go fishing one more time and become his Co-Pastor. I served as Co-Pastor in troubled times. There were several deaths in the church, but we kept the people encouraged in the Lord. I had to preach funerals of longtime members when he was lying in a hospital bed right next door in the church parsonage in brutal pain and we would have to call the ambulance and rush him back to the hospital. I saw many other people healed of all types of diseases as we changed his colostomy bag and cared for his wounds from his first and second surgeries. At this very time, I had to move out of my two bed room apartment into one bedroom. At one point I had my wife, my first born daughter, my son, and my new baby girl, my family of five, were all in one bedroom. Thank God five is the number of grace. God can even bring economic, as well true spiritual, revival in troubled times. I went to work. Took care of my responsibilities with the church and visited my father at the hospital in New York City.

God understands that He can revive us even in troubled times. During this challenge to my father's health, saints from all across the world believed for his healing. I confessed and stood on the word without wavering or any doubt. People that my father prayed for before he went into the hospital were being healed from all forms of cancer left and right. Even today, I still run into people who my father prayed for. They all received

227

miraculous healings from cancer. My father never received the physical manifestation of healing from the colon cancer which spread to his liver and throughout his stomach, but when he died he was with the Healer Himself, in the arms of Jesus. Yes, Jesus Christ is the Lord of Revival, even in the midst of troubled times.

Before my father died, my wife, Brenda, and I had our third child, Faith Miranda Mackey. And we bought our first house. He never got a chance to see that, but God did allow my father to witness the ground breaking to the new addition to the Mt. Sinai Baptist Church. The construction will literally double the size of the church building. He never had a chance to see the bulldozers on the site, and he never lived to see the walls erected or the roof put on, but in his wheelchair he saw the groundbreaking and shoveled the first scoop of dirt, and had the entire church to line up in seven separate lines representing the seven churches of Asia Minor. The preachers of the gospel and their wives were in the first line, then the deacons and deaconess in the second, then the trustees and their wives, then Sunday school, then missionaries, the music ministry, etc. He made sure everybody turned some dirt in Jesus' name.

When he was diagnosed, he came and hugged everyone in the church. He was tired and wanted to go home and be with Jesus, the Lord of revival even in troubled times. I believe that he wanted to be in the arms of Jesus, the great Fisher of men's lost souls. In fact, when my father was in the hospital in his worst condition, God gave me a song concerning God as a healer. Some folks may have lost love ones to sickness and disease, but healing is still ours. I don't know why everyone does not receive the physical manifestation of healing. But whether a saint receives healing on this side of glory or in the arms of Jesus up in heaven, God is still a healer. He was wounded for transgressions. He was bruised for iniquities. I know that healing is ours. Healing is the children's bread. I thank God for my father's life and the legacy that taught that God can revive, yes, even in troubled times. I knew that already, but now I know it at a much deeper level. In the hardest times, my entire family got closer to God even in the pain and the pressure. We walked by faith and not by sight.

In his book *Overcoming Disappointment,* Pastor Norman Lyons states that, "When trouble comes, it's not a good idea to stop walking. We must determine to walk through the trouble rather than mark time. The psalmist reminds us that God revives us in the midst of troubling times. Disappointment is a troubling time. God will not leave you hanging." [1]

Single parent, don't give up. God has revival just for you with your name on it even in troubled times. You, on the very brink of divorce, don't give up. God has real revival for you in troubled times. Divorced brother or sister, God has not forgotten about you. He will revive you in the midst of your trouble. Brothers and sisters who are right on the verge bankruptcy, God stills cares about you and he will revive you right in the very middle of your trouble. God is no respecter of persons, but He is a respecter of the principles of real revival. Get ready to go fishing, my brother and sister. God is going to send real revival in your worst troubled times. In the midst of my tears. In midst of my fears. Revive thy work, Lord. In the home. For the church. To impact the community. In his book, "The Purpose of Prasie and Worship," Dr. Myles Munroe states that, " Even when your life is full of problems, as it sometimes will be, others will notice that your response is different from that of other people and they'll ask you, 'Why aren't you afraid? How can you be so calm in the midst of such frightening circumstances?' You can reply, 'I'm not afraid because when troubles and problems come my way, I run to the dwelling place of my God through praise and I am safe.'"[2] Though we walk in the midst of trouble say this confession of faith: "Though I walk in the midst of threats, though I walk in the midst of persecution for Christ's sake, though I walk in the midst of trails and tribulations, God will revive me. He will stretch forth His mighty hand against my enemies, and His right hand will rescue me.

EPILOGUE

KEEP THE FIRES BURNING - FANNING THE FLAMES OF REAL REVIVAL

Our subject for this closing chapter, the Epilogue is: "Keep the Fire of Real Revival Burning." Think about that. Say it aloud, "Keep the Fire Burning." Meditate on that. Say it once for the Father, once for the Son, and once for the Holy Ghost, "Keep the Fire Burning."

In his book *Revival Fire,* Wesley Dewel wrote: "Our God is the God of revival. Revival is an essential part of His plan of redemption. From the time God created Adam and Eve and they fell into sin, Satan has tried to alienate humanity from God. He has tried to get us to disobey God and sever our relationship with Him."[1]

A Burning Desire To Fellowship with God

God has given us this. But how does one keep the fire of real revival burning amid all of the problems that are going on in life? Life is full of problems. Life is full of trials and tribulations. How do we survive? How do we overcome the obstacles that we face in difficult situations? How do we deal with the situations in which you say, "Where is God? I don't understand why He allows me to go through what He has allowed to go on in my life."

In the midst of all of this, the Word of God comes to us. In the book of Jeremiah we're going to read three different verses, Jeremiah 4:4; Jeremiah 20:9; Luke24:32.

Jeremiah 4:4 says, "Circumcise yourselves to the Lord, and take away the foreskins of your heart, ye men of Judah and the inhabitants of Jerusalem, lest My fury come forth like fire and burn that none can quench it, because of the evil of your doings."

Then let's look at Jeremiah 20:9, "Then I said, I will not make mention of him, nor speak any more in his name. But his word was in mine heart as a burning fire shut up in my bones; and I was weary in forbearing, and I could not stay."

And now Luke 24:32, "And they said one to another, Did not our hearts burn within us while He talked with us by the way, and while He opened unto us the scriptures?"

We're talking about "Keeping the Fire of Real Revival Burning." One of the first things that I want to emphasize is that we must have a heart correct with God. We must have a burning desire on the inside to get right with God. It has to be something that we really want, because we can say, "Lord, forgive me," but not deal with the real issues at hand. In the book *Power, Holiness and Evangelism: Rediscovering God's Purity, Power, and Passion for the Lost,* compiled by Randy Clark, Mr. Clark states that "during times of divine visitation by the Holy Spirit there have also been displays of power as seen through deep conviction of sin, which left the person in a state of spiritual anguish and deep sorrow for his sins until he became converted. The conviction would be so strong that people would be reduced to tears, sometimes weeping and wailing over their eternal separation from God. During the First and Second Great Awakenings, the Cane Ridge Revival, and other revivals in Church history, power encounters were seen when the unregenerate were supernaturally knocked to the ground, causing them to jerk or tremble under deep conviction."[2]

Getting to the Root of the Problem

We realize that the particular sin in our lives is only a by product of what is really the root of the problem--disobedience to God and letting sin have dominion over our lives, when God said, "Let not sin have dominion over you." We read in the book of Genesis how sin came into the earth. It was because of disobedience. It was because Adam and Eve took of the forbidden fruit and it caused the fall of man. And the by product of the fall of man was sin in the earth. The act was sin, for it was a by product of the act of disobedience due to deception.

We've got to get to the root of the problem and not let sin have dominion over us. And many times, things occur in our lives that we are not talking about. Many times things happen, maybe in our childhood, or in our adulthood, that we're not sharing in our testimonies. Many times, these are sins that you may have not committed, but the sin was done against you in the form of abuse.

Many times, things have occurred in our past that we're not telling anyone about, and we're acting out. We're doing things that we normally would not do, and saying, "Lord, forgive me." And God forgives us, but we go and do the same thing again, because we have not dealt with the root of the problem. We've got to deal with the sin that has dominion over us when it should not, according to the word of the Lord.

Sometimes, the root of the problem may have been the sin of verbal abuse, growing up in a home where maybe mamma or pappa said that you are no good. Or, you've heard an uncle or an aunt or friend of the family talking and they said that he or she was a mistake. They'll never get ahead or get anywhere in life. They'll never attain any prestige or wealth.

It may have been the sin of physical abuse, or someone may have taken you out in a back shed, and not only gave you a whipping, but did it to such an extent that they didn't want you to get back up again.

Or it may have been the sin of sexual abuse, incest or rape. It may have been so many things in life. Not just having someone there to care for us, not having someone to understand or have the compassion that is necessary for relationships in life, for us to grow, and for us to prosper, as individuals created in the image of God. But no matter the type of abuse, we've got to get to the root of the problem and receive God's inner healing day by day.

Dealing With Heartache and Pain

Jeremiah 4:4 says, "Circumcise yourselves to the Lord." That means, there are some things that God wants us to cut off. Just as the Jewish boys were circumcised when they were born, and even some older men, God wants us to cut off the root of the problem, the things that are blocking and hindering us from being all that God has called us to be.

It's not an easy thing. That's why it says, "Take away the foreskins of your heart." Where your treasure is, there your heart is also. God wants us to deal with the problems of our heart, not because we have not been freed, but because of things that we have on our mind that we have not processed. And since we haven't processed the things in our mind that have occurred in our life, we never can move on to getting our heart right. We've got to deal with our mind, and we've got to deal with our soul. We've got to deal with our pressure. We've got to deal with what causes the temptation and the yielding to it. It says, "Circumcise yourselves, and take away the foreskins of your heart."

God is calling for us to come correct with Him, to have that burning desire to live for Him in a closer way; to live for Him in a more intimate way, and that's what we're talking about when we say keep the fire burning. It doesn't mean that we are doing everything the way that it ought to be done, but it means that we're pressing towards the mark of the high calling which is in Christ Jesus. It means that we want to represent excellence, and when you have the burning desire to represent excellence, you begin to walk that way.

Keep Going

Oh, you might stumble. You might fall sometime, but God is there to pick you up. God is there to encourage you. I thank God for a Savior who is an encourager. I thank God for the Holy Spirit who is our Comforter. I thank God, He wants us to make it. Oh, He made us with faults. He made us with shortcomings, but that's what His grace is all about.

He tells us to circumcise ourselves before Him. It says, "Ye men of Judah and inhabitants of Jerusalem, lest My fury come forth like a fire that burns and none can quench it, because of your evil doings." There is a fire of God that represents judgment. There is a fire of God that represents His justice. We talk about the mercy of God and we talk about the grace of God, but God wants us to deal with the root of the problem. He says, "Circumcise the thing, I want you to deal with it day by day. I want you to deal with it moment by moment." And He says He wants to deal with it in the heart because He wants us to get the inner healing.

Inner Healing

Inner healing is an ongoing process. During Old Testament times, when a boy or man was circumcised they would be hurting for a long time. There may have been ointment to put on it, but there was also pain. If you don't get any pain, there is no progress. If you don't get any pain, there is no success. If you don't suffer with Jesus, you cannot reign with Him.

So when we say, "Keep the Fire Burning," it's not an easy thing. Let's look at Jeremiah as he goes on about struggling with things that had to be cut off in his own life.

Look at the 20th chapter, and the 9th verse. I'm so glad that the saints of God in the Bible admitted their shortcomings. In essence, they admitted they were not 100 percent perfect. But when we look at their lives, they share the testimony: "I've been through hell. I've been through high water, but God brought me out." Oh, it didn't happen over night, oh but yes, He did it. And if He can do it for them, He can do it for me; He can do it for you.

Don't Turn Back Despite The Trial

It says, "Then I said, I will not make mention of him, nor seek anymore in vain." That's the worse point that a preacher can get to. That's the worse point that a Sunday School teacher can get to. That's the worse point that a Bible study, or a deacon, or a trustee, or a member, or a choir member can get to. Oh, that's the worse point that a young man, a young woman, older men and older women can get to--that point where you say "I won't teach anymore in His Name." That point where you say, "I won't preach anymore in His Name." That point when you say, "I'm going to put the Bible in the box. I've had enough of God. I don't want to be bothered anymore."

Have you ever been to that point? Be honest. Have you ever gotten so discouraged that you said, "I'm not coming to that church anymore. I'm not singing on that choir anymore. I'm not dealing with those deacons... or that trustee... or that board anymore."

Have you ever been there? Oh, we don't live too far from Jeremiah's house. We've been to Jeremiah's 20 and 9 before. I've been there too many times. I have felt like turning back, but He gives us a key. I thank God for the hope that is in God's Word.

But His Word...

It says, "But His Word...." In spite of all the problems, *but*.... In spite of all the back biting, gossiping, bickering, in spite of being stabbed in the back, in spite of being called everything but a child of God, in spite of hell fire, in spite of discouragement, in spite of someone feeling like committing suicide, He says... "But...."

Oh thank God for "but".

"But His Word...." In my heart, there goes that word again. It is in the real essence of me, in my spirit man, burning as a fire, shut up in my bones.

Arthur L. Mackey, Jr.

I Can Feel the Fire

In the song "Revival Fire Fall" song writer Paul Balache says, "As we lift up your name, Let Your fire fall. Send Your wind and Your rain. On Your wings of love. Pour out from heaven. Your passion and presence and bring down Your burning desire."[3]

You may feel as though you don't want to sing a song anymore. You feel like you don't want to give a testimony anymore, but as you walk away from church, as you're trying to get away from what God has called you to do, there's a burning desire deep down within. It's now in your fingers. Too late to turn back now! There's a fire, and you can feel it in your ribs. There's a fire, and you can feel it in your toes. You can feel the fire of the Holy Ghost. When you lift up your hands, you can feel the fire in your elbows. The fire runs deep down in your soul, making you say you want to praise God. The presence of the Lord comes upon you like revival fire. That's why it's shut up in your bones. That's the central point that we have to declare in His Word. We must declare this without shame. We must declare it with confidence and a Holy boldness that's undeniably God. I'm going to preach His Word, whether it's to one, or whether it's to a thousand--preach His Word until the revival fire falls. Whether it's in Africa, or whether it's in America, I am not ashamed of the gospel because the gospel has the real revival fire, the good news.

So Much To Be Thankful For

He can give you inner peace. "He was wounded for our transgressions and he was bruised for our iniquities, the chastisement of His peace is upon us, and we are healed by His stripes." We are healed. I thank God for inner healing. I thank God for the peace that passes all understanding. I thank God for the Comforter. I thank God for the church.

I am often reminded of a poem that speaks dearly about the church: "The church is never a place, but always a people; never

236

a fold but always a flock; never a building but always a believers' assembly. The church is you who pray, not where you pray." --Anonymous.

Jesus, a Present Help

Luke 24:32 sets the scene: Some were following Jesus, walking down the old dusty road in deep depression because the Savior had been crucified. And now this is the third day. They heard that He had risen, but they haven't seen Him with their own eyes. As they walked down this dusty road, a traveler comes by. They begin to share with this traveler of how Jesus was crucified, of how their Savior is gone.

In the midst of their pain and depression, this man begins to preach to them, exhorting them and encouraging them. He told them to remember everything that God had done from the days of Moses--how He divided the Red Sea, how He was a pillar of fire by night, and a cloud by day, how He sent manna from heaven and fed them in the wilderness.

He talked to them about the great prophets, Jeremiah, Isaiah, Nehemiah, Zechariah, Malachi, Hezekiah, Nahum, Habakkuk and many others. And as He began to share with them how God had blessed the lives of their forefathers, their eyes were opened and they realized that it was Jesus walking with them.

Remember What Christ Has Done

I'm here to let you know that in the midst of our depression, in the midst of our discouragement, our lives are restored if we are walking with Jesus. He'll walk with us in the midst of the storm. He'll walk with us in the midst of financial hardships when we don't have the money to pay the bill. He's there walking with you. He's saying, "This, too, will pass." When you don't know how you're going to make it through the end of the month, or even through the end of the week, He's there to instruct you. This, too, will pass. He's there to remind us: "I brought your mamma out; I brought your daddy out; I brought your brother out; and I'm bringing you out. Remember I was a bridge over troubled water, I can do it again."

If we really want to get the inner healing, if we really want to keep the real revival fire burning, remember what God has already done and begin to give Him praise. Praising God will help keep the fire lit. We've got to learn to praise God in the midst of the pain. That's not the time to drop out. Your painful situation will be a testimony to somebody else.

Somebody's got a gun in their hand who feels like shooting himself. Your testimony might be able to throw that gun down, throw that crack down, throw that cocaine down. It's too far removed from us, it's just right around the corner, it's just right across the street.

Have a Talk with Jesus

Let's look at the scripture: "And they said one to another, Did not our heart burn within us while He talked with us by the way, while He opened unto us the scriptures?"

If you want to keep the fire burning, remember the preacher man said, "Talk with Jesus." That will work. Talk with Him while you're riding in the car. Talk with Him in the bathroom. Talk with Him while you're washing the dishes. Talk with Him while you're mopping the floor. Talk with Him while you're out taking a walk because there's a fight back home.

Have a little talk with Jesus; tell Him all about the trouble. He'll hear your very cry and He'll answer by and by. If we talk with Him, if you walk with Him on the lonely road, I'm sure that little spot will burn brighter and brighter everyday. Let the lower lights keep burning; send the beam upon the way. Some forsaken, struggling seamen you may rescue, you may save.

I thank God that He saved my soul 2000 years ago. I'm interested right now in saving some lives for Christ.

Give Your Problems to the Lord

In closing Leviticus 6:13 says, "The fire shall be burning for naught, and it shall then go out." And why is that? Because the book of Hebrews says, "Our God is a consuming fire."

Give your problems to God. Be honest about it, because our God can burn them up. But if we don't get to the root of the problem, nothing will ever change. If we're honest about it, have a talk with Jesus. Tell Him about all of your troubles. He will answer. I know because I laid it on the line and God made a way where there was no way.

You might have to give something up. It might mean that you'll be exposed in one way or the other, but if you lay it on the line, and you're honest with God, He'll make everything all right. Thank you, Lord.

Recently, I witnessed a tremendous move of God in London, England. During my visit to London, I was joined by Minister Kevin Delee, a respected member of the ministerial staff at Mt. Sinai Baptist Church and a good friend. The three day meeting was hosted by Pastor John Taylor, who was my room mate during my visit to the revival outpouring in Nigeria. Our spirits connected in Nigeria as we prayed together each day before we went to various part of Africa to preach the gospel.

Now there I was, getting off the plane in London's Heathrow Airport for three days of meetings that God literally transformed into a real revival, not just a three-day meeting. Well, before the first night of service, Minister DeLee, Pastor Taylor and I went into the conference hall, prayed in English and in the spirit over every single seat in the building.

By the time that meeting started a few hours later, the level of worship and praise was out of this world. When Pastor Taylor introduced me, I was led of the Holy Spirit to continue in worship. The presence of God was heavy in that intimate seating at England's Annon Court. You could look out the bedroom window and see sheep grazing on the pasture. By the time the

Arthur L. Mackey, Jr.

Holy Spirit allowed me to minister the message He gave for the congregation, He had already healed and delivered many people in the seats, on their feet, and on the floor. The Holy Spirit spoke personal, intimate, rhema words to each person at Annon Court as we worship and praised Him with our whole hearts.

Then there was a move of God, after the meeting, in our time of fellowship, in the dining room at the conference hall. We sang unto the Lord as though we were inebriated, for we were "drunk" in the Holy Spirit. Lives were dramatically changed through the awesome power of God.

Through revival fire, God brought inner healing into the lives of the people that Pastor John Taylor invited to the service. It became a wild fire that could not be put out. Wounds of the past were healed by the Master's hand. People were encouraged to fulfill their destiny in God. They were encouraged to anticipate that the best yet to come.

Yes, brothers and sisters throughout the world, the best is yet to come.

Face It The Days Of The Real Revival Are Not Over Yet!!!

1. **Truth Number One** - The year 2001 and then after is the third day.

   Evidence - Hosea 6:2 After two days he will revive us: in the third day he will raise us up, and we shall live in his sight.

   After two days (a day in the sight of the Lord is a thousand years) is the third day, the beginning of the third millennium since the life, death, and resurrection of Jesus Christ, at that is the very time, the very day in which we are living right now as you read this book. The word <u>after</u> gives no wiggle room. Many preachers and pastors from rich affluent communities claim that the days of revival are over, but the scripture says differently. Even in the 21st century, the new millennium, there is real revival power that is available to that backslidden Sunday school teacher and fallen prayer warrior who is a prostitute, the drug dealer who God created to really be a preacher of the Gospel of Jesus Christ, and etc. No, the greatest days of real revival will only begin to intensify right up until the rapture of the church. Remember, Christ is returning for a church without a spot or wrinkle. Only a major world wide revival could bring that about.

   2. Truth Number Two – The Biblical Pattern

   Evidence – Romans 14:9 For to this end Christ both died, and rose, and <u>revived</u>, that he might be the Lord both of the dead and living.

   Whatever has died must be revived by God in order to live again. Example- The resurrection of Lazarus, the resurrection of Jesus Christ, the rapture of the dead in Christ and the believers who remain on earth to meet Christ in the air.

3. **Truth Number Three** – Biblical Prophecy – The Greatest Revival Ever

Evidence – Joel 13:28 And it shall come to pass afterward that I will pour out my spirit upon all flesh: and your sons and daughters shall prophesy, your old men shall dream dreams, your young men shall see visions.

Acts 2:17 And it shall come to pass <u>in the last days</u>, saith God, I will pour out my spirit on all flesh: and your sons and daughters shall prophesy, and young men shall see visions, and your old men shall dream dreams.

GET READY CHURCH!!! THE BEST IS YET TO COME!!! In fact many people are experiencing personal and corporate revival right now!!! The Resurrection Revival, The Revival of Repentence, The Real Revival Revolution, The Third Day Revival, The Last Days Outpouring, and The Revival For The Rejected.

The reality is that the innercities, and the suburbs, uptowners and downtowners, and those who live in the pit or the penthouse, all drastically need a real revival touch from the presence of God in their lives that are in dire need of meaning, purpose and direction. As long as we or anyone else sins in any sense of the word, there will be a need for a revival of repentence.

PART 5:

THE MINISTRY

OF REVIVAL

Arthur L. Mackey, Jr.

Real Revival Words From the Bible

Châyâ-Revive-חזה

1.) Châyâ is the Hebrew translation of the word revive. Châyâ means to live, to be whole, to quicken, to save a life or lives, to make alive, to restore, repair, recover, and to nourish. Psalm 138:7, a Psalm of David, gives a classic example of Hebrew word Châyâ which means revive. "Though I walk in the midst of trouble, thou wilt revive me. thou shalt stretch forth thine hand against the wrath of mine enemies, and thy right hand shall save me." You could literally say that though I walk in the midst of trouble, thou wilt make me whole, restore me, repair me, recover me, nourish me, quicken me, and make me live.

Anazaō-Revived-

2.) Anazaō is the greek translation of the word revived. Anazaō means to recover life and to live again. The New Testament Book of Romans gives us both a negative and positive example of the word anazaō (revive). Therefore, proving that there is a revival of sin, as well as, a revival righteousness. It is our choice to choose which revival that we will be a part of. A.) <u>Sin can revive</u>- "For I was alive without the law once: but when the commandment came, sin revived, and I died. (Romans 7:9).

B.) <u>Christ can revive</u>- Now Romans 14:9 states that "For to this end Christ both died, and rose, and revived, that he might be Lord both of the dead and the living." Christ died, rose, and revived so that he would be the Lord of Revival who will ressurect the dead in Christ as well as those who are alive.

Michyâh-Reviving-

3.) Michyâh is the Hebrew translation of the word reviving. Michyâh means to experience the preservation of life, the quick, sustenance of God that bring recovery and preserves life. In every case, whether in the Old or New Testament, the words revive, revival, or reviving all point to the truth that recovery, restoration, ressurection life is found in the Lord Jesus Christ, The Lord of Revival.

Exra 9:8 declares that, "And now for a little space grace hath been shown from the Lord our God, to leave us a remnant to escape, and to give us a nail in his holy place, that our God may lighten our eyes, and give us a little reviving in our bondage."

Arthur L. Mackey, Jr.

4.) Revive (Châyâ), Revived (Anazaō), and Reviving (Michyâh)
The Cycle of Christian Life

Like the prophet Jeremiah God has also chose us before we were in out mother's womb. Our birth is a confirmation that God desired to revive His perfect plan for our lives that He decided before the foundations of the earth was laid. In this journey called life, we are in a cycle of life in which we ask God to revive us, and when He does we are revived, but yet since we are human, and finite, and not infinite or immortal, we still need a little reviving in our bondage. The greatest men and women of God all go through the Cycle of Christian life of asking God to revive us again that we might rejoice in You and because of this they are revived by the Master, but yet even the greatest Christian still falls short and needs a reviving again and again. You can fill your gas tank up once, but sooner or later you will need a refilling.

Revival Prayer For
Loneliness

Dear God, thank you for being there for me. Even when I am lonely I am never alone. For you will never leave me or forsake me. Dear God, give me strength to endure the pain of loneliness and enjoy my life, that you gave me, right now, today, in Jesus name, Amen.

Revival Prayer For
Inner Healing

Dear Father God, in the name of Your precious Son, Jesus Christ, touch my wounded spirit and tortured soul. I thank you for granting me a peace directly from You that passes all understanding. I receive the inner healing for my past present, and even my future in Jesus name, and thank you Lord for bringing essential wholeness and restoration into my life that was broken, battered, and bruised.

Revival Prayer For The Death of A Loved One

Heavenly Father, I have lost someone who was very dear to me to death. Help me to deal with death in a healthy manner. It is not easy God, and I will need your guidance to bring me through. I put my total trust in You that You will help me process the pain that this situation brings into my life. Thank you for helping me to process the anger so it does not become sin. Thank You Father for a God-given desire to praise Your name even in the midsts of the changes of life. In Jesus name. Amen.

Revival Prayer For The Divorced

Dear God, walk with me through the pain of the death of this relationship. Revive me and help me not to be eaten up with bitterness. Touch the life of my former mate and help me not to walk in hatred, but to bear forth the fruit of the Holy Spirit. Bring revival into both of our lives and minister to the chaos that brought about the divorced. Help us both to find help, healing, and wholeness in You.

Revival Prayer For Children

Dear God, Your Son, Jesus Christ, said to "suffer not the little children for such is the Kingdom of God." Touch the lives of the children. Bless them as they play, learn, and grow in the grace and Knowledge of our Lord and Saviour Jesus Christ. Amen.

<u>Revival Prayer For Teenagers</u>

Father God, in the name of Jesus, help me to deal with the challenges of being a teenager in the 21st Century. Help me Lord to deal with negative peer pressure such as smoking, drinking, drugs, and sex before marriage. Help me stand up and not give into negative peer pressure that can destroy my future. Amen.

Revival Prayer For Young Adults

Dear God, my Heavenly Father, lead me and guide me as I branch out in the new responsibilities that I have now in life. Help me be the best me that I can be through Your help Lord. In Jesus name I pray. Amen.

<u>Revival Prayer For Adults</u>

Dear God, thank you for letting me live long enough to reach adulthood. Help me to build my relationship with those whom You have placed in my life to be a witness to. Give me strength as I continue on this journey. In Jesus name. Amen

<u>Revival Prayer For Seniors</u>

Father God, in the name of Jesus, thank you for letting me live long enough to be a senior. Help me to reinvest what you have taught me over the years in the lives of others. Walk with me in times of sorrow and pain. Teach me to appreciate every single day that You give me. I will pour love into the lives of the children, because you have poured Your love into the life of this Your Child.

Arthur L. Mackey, Jr.

Revival Prayer For Married Couples

Dear God, You have made us one through marriage. Bind us together in mind and in spirit. Help me handle financial matter with wisdom and integrity. Help us to express our love daily in word and in deed. Teach us the true meaning of love in action. Help us not to be phony and draw us closer to You and to each other daily.

Revival Prayers For Business Decisions

Dear God, life is made up of decisions. Help me make the right choices in conducting business matters. I pray that I conduct no business that would bring shame to the representation of your name. Order my steps in Your word and I will give you all the glory, honor, and praise. Thank You Lord for leading me by your spirit to study and always be prepared to seek first the Kingdom of God. In Jesus name. Amen.

Arthur L. Mackey, Jr.

Revival Prayer For Financial Integrity

Father God, in the name of Jesus, teach me to obey You in the area of financial integrity. I will bring my tithe to the storehouse. I will invest wisely to secure a good future for me and my family. I will not eat up all of my money today, but I will put some aside for my rainy and my sunny days.

Revival Prayer For A Fall From Grace

Dear Father, please pick me up. With the help of Your outstretched hand I will rise up and stand again. I will get back up again, because revival is a better alternative than hell. I am sorry that I messed up, but thank you God for not giving up on me. In Jesus name. Amen.

Arthur L. Mackey, Jr.

<u>Revival Prayer For Physical Healing</u>

Father, your son, Jesus, was wounded for my transgression, bruised for my inequities, the chastisement of my peace was upon Jesus and with His stripes I am healed. I received your healing grace today in Jesus name from the top of my head to the soles of my feet. Amen.

Revival Prayer For The Baptism in the Holy Spirit

Father, baptize me in the Holy Ghost in Jesus name. Give me a prayer, praise, and worship language to pray out of love for the troubled, battered, broken, and bruised, with groanings that come only from the Holy Spirit, spread the love of Jesus through my life. In Jesus name. Amen.

Arthur L. Mackey, Jr.

Revival Prayer For Freedom From Drug Addiction I

Dear God I, need your help in resisting the temptation to take drugs. I pray for extra strength to stay clean. Help me to avoid people, places, and things that bring me into relapse. Give me strength that when I do run across old drug buddies that I will stand and not give in. Thank you for this grace to go on and not give up. In Jesus name. Amen.

Revival Prayer For Freedom For Drug Addiction II

Dear God, help me to resist the temptation to do drugs. Teach me to get high on the move of the Holy Spirit in my life. Help me not to go to the people, places, and things that build up the stronghold of drug addiction. Thank You God, that he whom the Son has set free is free indeed. Thank you for the Holy Ghost power to have a made up mind not to let drugs totally destroy my life. Dear God have your way in my life and teach me daily how to walk with You. In Jesus name. Amen.

Arthur L. Mackey, Jr.

Revival Prayer For Freedom From Alcoholism

Dear God, help me to respect my body as Your temple. Help me to resist the urge to drink Alcohol. Help me to deal with people, places, and things that attract me to Alcohol. I claim victory over Alcoholism in my life. Help me to get drunk in the Holy Spirit and not with wine, liquor or beer. In Jesus name. Amen.

Revival Prayers For Major Life Crisis Situations

Father God, in the name of Jesus, give me strength to make it through this storm of life. Draw me closer to you in the midst of this crisis. I am seeking your face for guidance. Dear God, thank You for being my shelter and my refuge. I lean, depend, and totally trust in You. In Jesus name. Amen.

Arthur L. Mackey, Jr.

Revival Prayer For the Sexually Abused

Dear God, touch my soul which yearns for help concerning the abuse that I have suffered. Touch my mind, will, and emotions that have carried this burden so long. I need your help God. Touch my body which has been violated in the worse way. Bring inner healing and essential wholeness into the broken, battered, and bruised areas of my life. And dear God, give me the strength to go on. With Your help I can make. I will be a surviver and a overcomer, because of Your help dear God. In Jesus name. Amen.

Revival Prayer For The Physically Abused

Dear God, my wounds are extremely deep. Some of my wounds and scars people can see and some are hidden from the eye, but You know my pain. You see all of my wounds and my deepest scars. Help me not to stay in this abusive situation. Give me the inner strength to get professional help. In Jesus name. Amen.

Arthur L. Mackey, Jr.

Revival Prayer For Single Parents

Dear God, I am raising my children alone and I need Your help. Help me be the parent that You would have me to be. Help me be there for my children. Fill the missing void in my life and in their life. Help me to depend upon You as my source of supply. I trust you to meet every need. Lead me by Your Holy Spirit and order my steps in Your word. In Jesus name I pray. Amen.

REVIVAL SONGS

"Revive Thy Work"
by Arthur L. Mackey, Jr.

Choir:

Ah,ah,ah,ah,ah,ah,ah

Ah,ah,ah,ah,ah,ah,ah

Lead:

O Lord, revive thy work in the midst of the years.

Choir:

Lord, revive us. Lord revive us.

Lead:

Please renew my spirit with brokenness and tears.

Choir:

Lord, revive us, Lord revive us.

Lead:

O Lord, revive my soul. Please cleanse and make me whole

Arthur L. Mackey, Jr.

Choir:

Revive thy work, Lord

Lead:

In the midst

Choir:

In the midst of the years.

Choir:

Ah,ah,ah,ah,ah,ah,ah
Ah,ah,ah,ah,ah,ah,ah

REVIVAL

Lead:

In the midst of my years, in the midst of tears,

Choir:

Revive Thy work, Lord.

Lead:

Yes. Send it, Jesus.

Choir:

Revival

Lead:

In the midst of my years, in the midst of tears,

Choir:

Revive Thy work, Lord.

Lead:

Yes,

Send it, Jesus

O,O,O, Revive.

Lead:

In the Home.

Choir:

Revive

Lead:

For the church.

Choir:

Revive.

Lead:

Impact the community.

Choir:

Help, we need revival!

Lead:

Yes, in the midst of my years,
In the midst of tears,

Choir:

Revive Thy work, Lord.

Lead:

Yes. Send it, Jesus.

Lead:

Revive Thy work, Lord.

Choir:

Revive Thy work, Lord.

Lead:

In the midst.

Choir:

In the midst of the years

Choir:

Ah,ah,ah,ah,ah,ah,ah
Ah,ah,ah,ah,ah,ah,ah

Together:

REVIVAL!

Arthur L. Mackey, Jr.

BREAK FORTH

By Arthur L. Mackey, Jr.

Choir:

Breakforth

Lead:

My friend, into singing.

Choir:

Cry loud.

Lead:

O God, in the midst of barrenness and desolation.

Choir:

Enlarge.

Lead:

Your tent. Prepare for the blessing.

Choir:

For you shall break forth.

Lead:

On the left and on the right.

276

Choir:

Your seed shall inherit.

Lead:

A greater blessing yet.

Choir:

Fear not.

Lead:

Neither be confounded.

Choir:

Fear not.

Lead:

Neither be ashamed.

Choir:

You shall

Lead:

Forget the shame of youth.

Choir:

And you shall not remember

Arthur L. Mackey, Jr.

Lead:

Your reproach anymore.

REACHING GENERATION X

By Arthur L. Mackey, Jr.

Lead:

There is a revival.

Choir:

Reaching generation X.

Lead:

For your survival.

Choir:

Reaching generation X.

Lead:

There is a revival, yeah.

Choir:

Reaching generation X
Lead:

For your survival, yeah

Choir:

Reaching generation X.

Arthur L. Mackey, Jr.

Lead:

We are the radical revival generation.

Choir:

Reaching generation X.

Lead:

We are a holy nation.

Choir:

Reaching generation X.

Lead:

We come in prayer and consecration.

Choir:

Reaching generation X.

Lead:

Yes we do. Praise the Lord.

Choir:

Praise the Lord, reaching generation X.

Lead:

Thank you, Jesus.

Choir:

Thank you, Jesus, reaching generation X.

Lead:

Hallelujah.

Choir:

Hallelujah, reaching generation X

Arthur L. Mackey, Jr.

ENDNOTES

Introduction

1 David Bryant, *Prisoners of Hope,* in *New Man Magazine,* page 30. Strang Communications, Lake Mary, Florida, Sept. 1996.

2 Lane, Vann, *Children of Revival,* Revival Press, Shippensburg, Pa., p. 129, 1998

3 Wirt, Sherwood E., *Jesus, Man of Joy,* Thomas Nelson Publishers, Nashville, Tennessee 1991, pg. 150.

4 Proctor, Samuel Dewitt, *The Substance of Things Hoped For—a Memoir of African-American Faith,* Putnam, New York, 1995, p. xviii.

5 Engle, Lou, *Digging the Wells of Revival,* Revival Press, Shippensburg, Pa., 1998. 0. 44.

6 *The Words of Martin Luther King, Jr.,* Newmarket Press, New York, 1983, pg. 17.

7 Carson, Ben, M.D., *Think Big: Unleashing Your Potential For Excellence.* Zondervan Publishing house, Grand Rapids, Michigan 1992, pg. 244.

8 Meyer, Joyce, *Help Me I Married,* Harrison House, Tulsa, Oklahoma 2000, pp. 305-6.

9   Ron McIntosh, "The Quest for Revival-Experiencing Great Revivals of the Past, Empowering You For God's Move Today!" Harrison House, Tulsa, OK, 1997, pg 9

10   Winkie Pratney, "Revival-Its Principles and Personalities-Twenty Centuries of Vision and Visitation", Huntington House Publishers, Lafayette, Louisiana, 1994, pg 23

11 Duewell, Wesley, *Revival Fire,* Zondervan Publishing House, Grand Rapids, Michigan, 1995, pg. 11.

Chapter One

1   Pratney, Winkie, *Revival: Its Principles and Personalities, Twenty Centuries of Vision and Visitation* (Lafayette, Louisiana: Huntington House, 1994), p. 15

2   Hanby, Dr. Mark, *Anointing the Unsanctified—An Unveiled Revelation In Spiritual Authority,* Destiny Image, Shippensburg, Pa., 1993 p. 120

3   Seary, George, *Revival Us, Lord,* Integrity's Praise Music/BMI, 1994

4   Munroe, Myles, *The Burden Of Freedom-Discover The Keys To Your Individual, Community, And National Freedom,* Creation House, Lake Mary, Florida, p. 6, 2000.

5   Ravenhill, Leonard, *Lord, Send a Revival (Poem)*

6   Ravenhill, Leonard, *The Revival Song (Poem)*

7   Mackay, William P. *Revive Us Again* (Classic Hymn)

Chapter Two

1   Porter, Bishop Philip H., *Better Men on the Path to Purity,* Zondervan Publishing House, Grand Rapids, Michigan, 1998, p. 168

2   Spring, Howard, *Revival Quotes Archive* www.lifeaction.org/archives/archive *revival quotes htm*

Chapter Three

1   *Revival,* by John Avant, Malcolm McDow, and Alvin Reid, Editors, Broadman & Holman, Publishers, Nashville, Tennessee 1996, p. 176. Afterword by Bill Bright

2   Ravenhill, Leonard, *Revival Praying,* Bethany House Publishers, Minneapolis, Minnesota, 1962-1996

3   Hanby, Dr. Mark, *Anointing the Unsanctified,* p. 101

4   *Family–How To Have A Healthy Christian Home,* Compiled and Edited by Hal Donaldson, Ken Horn, Ann Floyd, and Joel Kilpatrick, Pentecostal Evangel Books, Published by Gospel Publishing House, Springfield, Missouri, p. 67, 1999

Chapter Four

1   Pickett, Fushia, *How To Receive Revelation From God,* (Charisma, Lake Mary, Florida 2/19/97, p. 67)

2   Taylor, Dr. Gardener, Ed Gilbreathe, *America's Dean of Preachers,* Christianity Today, 12/11/95, p. 67

3   Long, Bishop Eddie, *The New Revival In America,* General Editor, Dr. Edwin Louis Cole, Manpower—The

Call to African-American Men for Spiritual Revival Thomas Nelson Publishers, Nashville, Tennessee, 1997, p. 26

4   Long, Bishop Eddie, *The New Revival In America,* General Editor, Dr. Edwin Louis Cole, Manpower—The Call to African-American Men for Spiritual Revival, Thomas Nelson Publishers, Nashville, Tennessee, 1997, p. 26

Chapter Five

1   Warren, Rick, *The Purpose Driven Church–Grwoth Without Compromising Your Message and Mission,* Zonolervan Publishing House, Grand Rapids, Michigan, p.20, 1995

2   Keefauver, Larry, *Azusa Street Devotional,* Azusa Street Devotional, Lake Mary, Florida, Creation House, 1997

Chapter Six

1   *Manpower—The Call to African-American Men for spiritual Revival,* General Editor Dr. Edwin Louis Cole; Bernard, Rev. A.R., "The Culture of Christianity" (Thomas Nelson Publishers, 1997, p. 148, Chapter 13, "The Culture of Christianity."

2   Winkie, Pratney, *Revival, Its Principles and Personalities, Twenty Centuries of Vision and Visitation,* Huntington House Publishers, Lafayette, Louisiana, p. 15, 1994

Chapter Seven

1 Finney, Charles G.: *Principles of Revival* (Bethany House Publishers, Minneapolis, Minnesota, 1987, p. 22)

Chapter Eight

1 Duewel, Wesley, *Revival Fire,* Zondervan Publishing House, Grand Rapids, Michigan, 1995, pg. 26

2 Ray, Rev. Dr. Sandy F., *Journeying Through A Jungle,* Broadman Press, Nashville, Tennessee, p. 67, 1979

3 Cole, Dr. Edwin Louis, General Editor: *Manpower—The Call To African-American Men for Spiritual Revival,* Long, Bishop Eddie: The New Revival In America (Nashville, Tennessee, Thomas Nelson Publishers, 1997), p. 26

Chapter Nine

1 Mackey Jr., Arthur L.: *Walking Through the Doorways of Destiny* (Lanham, M.D.: Pneuma Life Publishing, 1997), p. 5. Foreword by Elder Donnie McClurkin.

2 Thomas, B. Carlisle R., *Shades of Grace,* Diadem Music Group, Inc., Nashville, Tennessee p. 96

3 Spurgeon, Charles Haddon, *A Real and Lasting Revival* (www.spurgeon.org)

4 Murray, Andrew: *Revival Quotes Archive* (www.lifeaction.org/archives/Archive_Revival quotes htm)

5   Jakes, Bishop T.D.: *Anointing, Fall on Me: Accessing the Power of the Holy Spirit* (Lamhem, M.D.: Pneuma Life Publishing, 1997), p. 5

Chapter Ten

1   Anderson, Neil T. & Towns, Elmer L.: *Rivers of Revival* (Regal, Ventura, California 1997) p. 15

Chapter Eleven

1   King, Rev. Bernice A.: *Hard Questions, Heart Answers* (Broadway Books, New York, 1996, p. 64

Chapter Thirteen

1   Lyons, Norman Jr., *Overcoming Disappointment,* Chapter 7, *Revival in the Midst of Trouble, LHP, p. 31, 1999*

2   Munroe, Dr. Myles, *The Purpose And Power Of Praise And Worship, Destiny,* Image Publisher, Inc., Shippensburg, Pennylvania, p. 52, 2000

Epilogue

1   Duewell, Wesley, *Revival Fire,* Zondervan Publishing House, Grand Rapids, Michigan 1995, p. 25

2   Clark, Randy, *Power, Holiness and Evangelism,* Destiny Image, Shippensburg, Pa. 1999 pg. 56

3   Balache, Paul, *Revival Fire Fall,* 1996, Integrity's
     Hosanna Music/ASCAP)

Arthur L. Mackey, Jr.

The Sinner's Prayer

The First Step Toward True Success

Father God, in the mighty, marvelous and matchless name of Jesus, I come crying out before Your eternal throne of grace, realizing that the place where I am right now has become my mourner's bench of sorrow and repentance.

Heavenly Father, I am asking You to forgive me of all my sins, faults, lies, misdirected desires, and shortcomings. I accept as an undeniable fact today that over 2,000 years ago on Calvary's old rugged cross, Jesus Christ of Nazareth washed away my sins and removed them from me as far as the east is from the west. That is an infinite line that never stops. That is how far my personal, public, and private sins have been thrown away. They have now been literally cast down into the sea of forgetfulness.

I personally proclaim at this very moment that Jesus Christ lived, died and rose again that I might receive true success called salvation. Today I accept, confess, and believe deeply within that Jesus Christ is the liberating Lord of my life and the satisfying Savior of my soul.

Now, Lord, I ask You to lead, guide and direct me by the Holy Spirit from one degree of grace unto another. And while I am on this journey of new growth, learning, and Christian development, teach me, heavenly Master, how to walk day by day in the footsteps of Your Son, Jesus Christ, Amen

*Name*_____

*Date*_____

291

Arthur L. Mackey, Jr.

Index

REVIVAL ART WORK

Arthur L. Mackey, Jr.

Arthur L. Mackey, Jr.

Arthur L. Mackey, Jr.

REVIVAL NOTES

_____

_____

_____

_____

_____

_____

_____

_____

_____

_____

_____

REVIVAL NOTES

Arthur L. Mackey, Jr.

REVIVAL NOTES

_____

_____

_____

_____

_____

_____

_____

_____

_____

About the Author

Rev. Arthur L. Mackey, Jr. is the Pastor of Mt. Sinai Baptist Church Cathedral in Roosevelt, N.Y., and Founder and President of Arthur Mackey Ministries and Vision of Victory Ministries. Rev. Mackey is also the author of *Walking Through The Doorways Of Destiny*, *Inner Healing For Men*, *Inner Healing For Women*, and *Real Revival*. He lives in Freeport , N.Y. with his wife, Brenda, and three children, Yolanda, Jordan, and Faith.

Books Written by Arthur L. Mackey, Jr.

 The Biblical Principals Of Success (Pneuma Life Publishing)

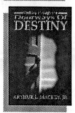 Walking Through The Doorways Of Destiny (Pneuma Life Publishing)

 Inner Healing For Men (Pneuma Life Publishing)

 Inner Healing For Women (Pneuma Life Publishing)

 Real Revival (E-Book) (1st Books Library)

Real Revival (Softcover) (1st Books Library)

Real Revival (Hard Cover) (1st Books Library)

For additional copies of **Real Revival:**
(soft cover, hard cover, e-book)

Call **1 (888) 280-7715** or visit your local bookstore.

To contact **Pastor Arthur L. Mackey, Jr.**

Write:

Mount Sinai Baptist Church Cathedral
243 Frederick Avenue
Roosevelt, NY 11575
www.mtsinaibcc.org

Printed in the United States
141151LV00001B/282/A

9 780759 605848